RECLAIMING STYLE

RECLAIMING STYLE

USING SALVAGED MATERIALS TO CREATE AN ELEGANT HOME

BY MARIA SPEAKE & ADAM HILLS OF RETROUVIUS

WORDS BY HETTIE JUDAH

PHOTOGRAPHY BY DEBI TRELOAR

LONDON · NEW YORK

First published in 2012 by
Ryland Peters & Small
20–21 Jockey's Fields
London WC1R 4BW
and
519 Broadway,
5th Floor
New York, NY 10012
www.rylandpeters.com

Text © Maria Speake and Adam Hills 2012
Design and photography
© Ryland Peters & Small 2012

A CIP record for this book is available from
the US Library of Congress and the
British Library.

10 9 8 7 6 5 4 3 2 1

Senior designers Megan Smith and Paul Tilby
Commissioning editor Annabel Morgan
Location research Jess Walton
Production Patricia Harrington
Art director Leslie Harrington
Editorial director Julia Charles

ISBN: 978-1-84975-267-1

Printed in China

RPS CICO BOOKS

For digital editions visit
rylandpeters.com/apps.php

CONTENTS

INTRODUCTION

OPPOSITE AND THIS PAGE These mahogany cupboards in the Retrouvius warehouse were salvaged from the Natural History Museum in London. About 350 of them had become surplus to requirements when their contents were moved to the new Darwin Centre. Made by Howard & Sons, the Victorian joinery work is of an outstanding quality. The cupboards are about the size of a double kitchen unit and have been used as such by a number of Retrouvius's clients. In front of the cupboards (opposite) stands a pitch pine bench salvaged from a church.

Nestled between junk shops and Brazilian cafés on an ungentrified West London street, the Retrouvius warehouse is an unlikely destination. But for design insiders, this cavernous, L-shaped emporium, stretched over multiple storeys between two buildings, has become something of a cult address.

Inside, the stock ranges from elegant reupholstered sofas and pretty mirrors to stacks of limestone cladding and heavily graffitied school desktops. There is always something unexpected – a vast Art Deco bathroom set, an antique optometrist's table or science laboratory taps – and everything has a story.

BOTTOM AND BELOW
Salvaged materials in
their raw state. These
iroko laboratory tops
have just arrived in the
material storage area
straight off a building site.

At the heart of Retrouvius is the belief that good materials and well-made things are precious; whether quarried stone or a piece of expert joinery, these objects were hard won and have an intrinsic value that argues for them to be reconditioned and intelligently reused. Much of the stock that makes its way into the warehouse might otherwise have ended up in landfill or as bonfire fodder, but as the design projects presented in this book so beautifully demonstrate, good salvaged materials can yield astonishing results if treated with care, style and an adventurous spirit.

Founded twenty years ago by partners Adam Hills and Maria Speake when they were studying architecture in Glasgow, Retrouvius began as a way to help conserve the Victorian tenement buildings in the city's reinvigorated West End. "My first eureka moment was when I realized that, because the West End of Glasgow is very homogenous architecturally, you could remove the doors and shutters and fireplaces from a building that Glasgow University was demolishing and use them in a building two or three streets away and they would fit, physically and historically," explains Adam.

Quite quickly the scope of the company grew, from salvaged oddments from Victorian tenements, through selling church pews to pubs and stained-

RIGHT AND OPPOSITE This stack of dismantled cinema seats came from a Methodist church that had been destroyed during the Second World War, and subsequently rebuilt at the end of the 1940s. During the post-war period, people tended to use whatever they could lay their hands on, hence finding cinema seats in a church. About 200 of them were salvaged in very good condition. The cast-iron supports for the seats are visible towards the back of the picture (opposite). Retrouvius reconditioned the seats and divided them into shorter rows to make them more suitable for domestic or commercial use, selling them off in little sets of three or four.

ABOVE Looking over this rack of doors at the warehouse, Adam confesses that sometimes he perhaps takes too much pity on things that need to be saved. "Some of them are nice, but others I shouldn't have bothered with."

glass windows to Japanese wedding chapels, to a more generalized interest in materials and reuse. Since moving to London in 1997, Adam and Maria's practice has gradually diverged along the two complementary fields of design and salvage. In a way, the design projects started as a means to demonstrate what could be done with their stock; many architects and builders were nervous about working with materials that might require special treatment, or for a job to have to accommodate components that came in non-standardized sizes.

Adam explains how important it is to choose the right builders to work on a job using salvaged materials. "Sometimes clients will come in wanting to use old wood, for example, then phone up sheepishly a week later saying that they can't buy it because their builder refuses to touch it. You definitely have to find someone who's sympathetic to using it. Salvage is much harder work than just bunging in new stuff, and it's not necessarily cheaper."

Adam now takes on just about any good material that could be used in making a building, as well as all manner of apparently random oddments that he thinks might appeal to his clientele. "Once you've got your mind tuned to saving stuff, and to salvage and materials and quality, you are always thinking laterally – it's just a case of seeing what's there and putting it in a new context," he explains.

BELOW LEFT These hardwood laboratory tops are popular as kitchen surfaces. Some clients sand them down to expose the rich grain of the wood, while others prefer to leave the scuffs and graffiti of their previous life visible.
RIGHT These oak handrails came from the old London School of Economics building in Lincoln's Inn, London.
BELOW LEFT A stack of handmade paper destined for a folio edition of Shakespeare was rejected because of misprints. Adam and Maria now use it as wallpaper.
BELOW RIGHT Fabric sample books salvaged from a gentlemen's cloth merchant.

"You always approach a building with first principles, by asking what it's made out of. A lot of people would look at something like Heathrow Airport's Terminal 2 and think that, because it's a hideous building, there can't be anything valuable inside it. Whereas in fact you can go inside a bit of Brutalist architecture and look up the stairs and realize that the handrail is made out of a solid piece of hardwood, or that there's an incredible floor or interesting light fittings. You have to ignore the hideous surroundings and think of these things in a different environment. The whole principle of antiques dealing is to take something from where it's not appreciated to somewhere that it is."

Among other things, Adam bought 200 tonnes of Derbyshire fossil limestone from Heathrow's Terminal 2 building before it was demolished. This distinctive stone is patterned with the fossilized remains of seashells, and is strongly associated with post-war British architecture. That batch of stone can be seen in many of the interiors in this book. Working with salvage makes you appreciate the finite availability of materials: 200 tonnes may sound like a lot, but the fossil limestone has all been sold. The design projects that feature that batch of stone made use of a lovely material with a very particular architectural history that was only available during a narrow window of time. Once it's gone, it's gone.

ABOVE LEFT Moulded timber frames await sale or reuse.
ABOVE RIGHT These enamel panels with dainty chinoiserie decoration are destined to be used in one of Maria's design projects, as are the unusually shaped brackets in front of them.
FAR LEFT These snooker table legs are turned mahogany, and have been used for coffee tables and even beds. Adam bought a quantity of snooker tables, which turned out to be easier to sell as parts (in particular the slate, which makes excellent countertops) rather than assembled.
OPPOSITE Fossil limestone salvaged from Terminal 2 of Heathrow Airport clads one of the walls in the warehouse.

Adam is often alerted to salvage sites by demolition contractors (although he has also been known to happen upon buildings just as work was commencing on them as he was going past on his scooter), and he then only has a day or two to assess what can be removed and take it off site. Many demolition sites, particularly in London, won't even let salvage merchants in for that long because their construction schedules are so tight – the amount of usable materials and fittings that end up in landfill as a result is astronomical.

While there is, of course, a strong environmental aspect to their work, conservation is so fundamental to the Retrouvius ethos that any 'green' credentials are almost accidental. Adam and Maria both have a deeply ingrained dislike of waste, and a desire to do the best they can with what's available to them. Many of the clients whose homes feature in this book tell stories of Maria tirelessly moving and reworking their existing furniture until it sits happily in a new space. Nothing gets thrown away.

Visitors to the warehouse range from home owners looking for unusual pieces and clients involved in renovation projects to fashion stylists searching out props and owners of some of London's most fashionable bars and restaurants tracking down décor for their latest venture.

Maria treats the materials that she uses as if the client is their custodian rather than their final owner; everything from stone to parquet is installed with an eye to its one day being reused in another space. It's a practice that one client made use of sooner than expected, moving the marble cladding of their bathroom from one property to another.

The projects featured in this book have all been completed within the last three years and all of them possess the distinctive Retrouvius house style. It's not about using reclaimed pieces to recreate a purist period décor, but instead mixing salvaged materials with pieces from different eras and with a modern aesthetic. Her work with these materials results in domestic interiors a richness and sense of long use and care. The materials have a soul to them not available in the contemporary equivalent.

OPPOSITE The cinema seats seen on pages 8–9 have been reconditioned and assembled for display in the warehouse. In front of them hangs a trio of green enamel factory lampshades and a Eero Saarinen tulip table.
LEFT These massive copper roof ventilators also come from the demolished London School of Economics and were made by Ewart's of Euston Road.
ABOVE LEFT A 1950s chair awaits a makeover.
ABOVE RIGHT The façade of the warehouse was put together from copper light windows salvaged from the University of the Arts building near Bond Street.

BARBICAN MODERN

Situated within a landmark development in central London, the corridor-style format of this 1970s apartment made for a tricky living space. The redesign focused on generating warmth and atmosphere while creating a stylish interior that nodded both to the clients' Italian roots and the cultural significance of the building itself.

Before the redesign, the focus of this apartment was its spectacular views. Set on the twenty-ninth floor of a tower on the Barbican Estate, it looks out over London both ancient and modern, from St Paul's Cathedral to the Swiss Re building, but it felt less like a home than a viewing station. The original scheme had centred on uncluttered, minimalist furniture in a style that the clients wryly refer to as 'British Airways' First Class lounge' and which only accentuated the harder and more forbidding aspects of the Barbican Estate's architecture. With so much attention being pulled outwards, there was a lack of homely comfort and little of the space within was being used.

THIS PAGE AND OPPOSITE
Inspiration for the style of this interior was taken from elements that were very much part of the clients' lives within the space. The coloured spines of their antique books (opposite) were used as the source for the rich, rusty colours of the rugs and upholstery fabrics, the effect of which can be seen most dramatically in the custom upholstery of the sofa. The slim curves of the clients' Italian standard lamp to the right of the bookshelves have been echoed in the choice of elegant mid-century Italian furniture, and bespoke pieces such as the dining table (above), which was made with salvaged hardwoods that complement the tones of the parquet screen.

ABOVE The deep red hue used on the sliding doors of the dining room and in a strip along the bottom of the wall cabinets in the galley kitchen was inspired by the colours of the vintage flatweave rug beneath the dining table. The 1954 JL Møller Model 75 chairs were upholstered in a combination of red leather – salvaged from Dunhill – and neutral linen to stop things looking too coordinated.

LEFT At the start of the project, all of the clients' furniture was moved out of the space and a selection of mid-century pieces brought in and arranged in a variety of different configurations to see how the space could be transformed and used in a number of different ways. Books are very much at the heart of this home, so warm, relaxing spaces to sit and read were a priority, as was an elegant dining room for guests.

LEFT AND BELOW This 1950s boomerang-shaped coffee table does not have any kind of maker's mark on it. The top of the table – which includes an aperture for a pot plant – features a combination of mosaic and larger tiles, the subtle colours of which were taken as the inspiration for the tones of the upholstery in this part of the living room.

OPPOSITE The curvy brass-legged 1950s Carlo De Carli lounge chair came as part of a suite with the sofa and one of the chairs shown on the previous page. The sofa was reupholstered in cotton piqué, while the two chairs were covered with a wool and linen mix in shades of rose and sand that echo the tiled tabletop.

In order to create welcoming living areas, and steal some of the focus away from the windows, the main space was divided into three interlinked sections by a monumental set of sliding walls faced in salvaged parquet. Taken from the floor of a primary school where it had fallen into poor condition after many years of heavy use, the parquet was in the form of thin overlay strips that made it light enough to use in this way. After careful reconditioning the rich shades of the aged tropical hardwood really shone out, and brought some much-needed warmth and colour into the heart of the apartment.

New furniture was brought in throughout the apartment, most of it mid-century Scandinavian and Italian. Before the final furniture selection was made, the apartment was treated like a blank canvas and pieces were moved into

various different configurations to see how the space might function best. Even when working with the furniture that you already have, moving pieces around and trying new arrangements is an effective way to get the most out of a space.

Vintage Turkish and Moroccan rugs were used to soften the space and provide little islands of focus. While some were in colours that the clients found a little alarming at first, they worked well with the tones of the wood and the spines of the antique books that line the living room. Both the rugs and the books provided inspiration for the upholstery textiles in the central living space.

The kitchens on the Barbican Estate were all custom built by the yacht design company Brooke Marine, the logo of which can still be seen stamped into the metalwork. Designed for maximum efficiency of space, the kitchens are positioned towards the back of the apartments in the belief that no one using them would have much need of natural light. The set-up invariably evokes a rather unreconstructed 1960s tableau in which the

OPPOSITE Each block of reclaimed parquet was individually sanded before positioning to ensure an uneven finish that reflects the light and shows the tones of the wood to best effect. Part of the skill of designing with salvaged materials is to have the vision to imagine how those materials might be transformed – in this case, how old scuffed floors could become a sculptural feature at the heart of a sophisticated apartment.
LEFT This elegant 1950s Italian sideboard and mirror were sourced for the clients by Retrouvius.

ABOVE Art plays a significant role in the life of this flat. The clients offered up favourite images by collagist and installation pioneer Kurt Schwitters, and Vilmos Huszár, one of the founders of the De Stijl movement, as inspirations for the redesign.

LEFT AND FAR LEFT The palette for the guest bedroom was taken from a strip of salvaged Anatolian silk used as a feature panel on a set of curtains. The colours of the silk panel are echoed by the vintage Indian bedspread.
BELOW The focal point of the master bedroom is a Turkish flatweave rug used to cover the headboard.
OPPOSITE When the Barbican Estate was built, the bathrooms were tiled, both wall and floor, in a rather stark arrangement. The new bathroom is lined in reclaimed iroko hardwood and fossil limestone, but uses the original niches and storage spaces of the original design, as well as fixtures taken from the Barbican's own salvage depot.

husband relaxes contentedly in the sitting room while the wife slaves over supper in a cramped, windowless kitchen. Although perhaps a little outdated in its design, the kitchen does work well, and was left untouched save for a strip of deep red painted along one side, which pulls it together with the dining room beyond.

A salvage store was set up on the estate a few years ago by residents keen not to waste the Barbican's bespoke fixtures and fittings, and it has a fluctuating stock of everything from door handles to kitchen units. For this renovation, the depot provided an invaluable supply of items like ceiling roses that had been removed by previous tenants.

It was actually the Barbican Estate's notoriously clinical bathrooms that originally led the clients to commission the entire new design for their home. Previously clad entirely in white tiles, and with an inaccessible high-sided shower tray that doubled up as a bidet (a fellow resident has described the experience of using the shower as "like sluicing down in an abattoir"), after forty years of use they were starting to feel grubby. Having been replaced by more modern and user-friendly pieces in an en-suite shower and master bathroom, the original sanitary fixtures were returned to the Barbican Estate's in-house salvage depot ready to be renovated and used elsewhere.

This terraced house in North London was redesigned to meet the needs of a gregarious family with three children. The house had to be practical enough for daily life, but with an edge of glamour that reflected the exuberant personalities of the occupants.

CANALSIDE HOUSE

Stepping in through the front door, a boldly striped carpet draws your gaze up the stairs to the subtle milk chocolate swoops of the wallpaper. Straight ahead, you look across the rich salvaged parquet floor of the kitchen, inlaid with a 'rug' of hand-cut Moroccan tiles, through French doors to the sunny garden behind. Generous glass-inlaid sliding doors to your left lead into an elegant drawing room laid out ready for an evening of music and cocktails. Instinctively you get a sense of the multiple forces at play within this household – *joie de vivre* and practicality, a warm family home and an inviting place for guests of all ages.

In many ways this project personifies Maria's ongoing goal of creating "a riposte to the joylessness and seriousness and masculinity" that bedevil most people's experience of working with architects. The house is full of unexpected elements, from glamorous lighting fixtures to pieces of stained glass and laser-etched wooden panels. "People have to add their own layer to a space," she explains. "But you allow people to inhabit the fantasy of who they want to be – to be more indulgent and take the things that give them pleasure." In this design ethos, the house is a platform for its inhabitants and the interior expresses the intermingling of their different personalities.

The current owners had originally lived in the two downstairs flats and bought the upper part of the building when it became available and as their family expanded. As it was reborn as a family home, the house was extensively remodelled, including the entrance hall, the opened-out

THIS PAGE AND OPPOSITE
Leading directly off the entrance hall, this simple but elegant sitting room was originally the kitchen. The vintage gramophone beckoning from centre stage hints at the possibility of a cocktail party kicking off at any second, and lets us know that this is very much a room designed for entertaining. The décor was left deliberately unfussy, right down to the cool green upholstery on the French chairs, to keep the focus of the room on the people in it and (fingers crossed) their fabulously decorative outfits. The patterned chair just glimpsed behind the sliding doors (above right) is upholstered in one of the client's own distinctive tweed designs.

living spaces and a newly installed staircase. Salvaged flooring, doors and fittings helped to keep the basic elements of the interior harmonious with the original architecture and have been ingeniously combined with more contemporary elements.

At the heart of the redesign was the aim of enabling the building to resume its previous grandeur. The staircase had been boxed in on the upper levels, so the entrance hall had lost its sense of soaring space. A lack of storage and easily negotiated doorways on the ground floor left the hall cluttered with bicycles, toys and pushchairs. Opening out the ground floor, creating storage space and exposing the upper levels of the staircase allowed the entrance to feel spacious and welcoming again.

Entertaining is a way of life in this home. "There's no point having a beautiful house if you don't invite people round," says the client. "There's no point worrying about things and fussing – here you just polish everything afterwards and the scuffs add to the atmosphere." As many of Retrouvius's clients note, one advantage to using salvaged materials in an interior is the slightly *laissez-faire* attitude that comes with them. On the one hand, the materials already show the signs of wear and use, but on the other, because they are solid and high quality, they tend to be much more enduring than their modern equivalents.

THIS PAGE AND OPPOSITE Leading off the airy sitting room shown on the previous pages, the practical grey-fronted modern units of this kitchen have been pepped up by the addition of salvaged drawer fronts running in vertical and horizontal strips. These are practical as well as decorative – not only do they face the kitchen drawers but the handle on the vertical strip opens the fridge. The hardwood on the unit top and on the central island originally came from a school science laboratory.

To accommodate the constant flow of people in and out of the house, the ground and lower ground floors were designed with multiple routes through the space. The hinged doors leading off the hallway were replaced by pocket sliding doors, all made with salvaged materials. Doors with glazed panels were chosen to increase the flow of light. When open, the large doorways and uncluttered hall space made it easier for bulky items like bicycles to come right through into the kitchen to be stored on the newly created balcony beyond it.

Originally the stairs to the basement ran beneath the main stairwell and were accessed from the entrance hall. While this is a common arrangement in Victorian houses, it tends to result in dark and poky staircases, and a basement that feels detached from the action elsewhere in the home. With this in mind, the old staircase was removed and a wide, easily negotiated new one built leading off the family kitchen-dining room.

When engaging in major structural projects such as this one, Maria tries to reuse as much material as possible – existing materials help to dictate the palette of a project and suggest which materials should logically be employed in the rest of the design. In this case, all the wood from the old stairs was saved and reused, together with salvaged parquet, oak floorboards and panels and hardwood worksurfaces.

The colour scheme selected for the house combines deep, dusty tones and a cooler palette. This can be seen, for example, in the contrast between the boldly coloured stripes on the stair carpet and the more restrained tones of the wallpaper. This combination of colour and pattern was inspired by the clients, whose personal styles marry elegant pragmatism with bohemian verve. In some areas, this dynamic aspect is made explicit; in others, the textiles and colours have been left relatively plain, allowing the personalities of the clients to take centre stage.

OPPOSITE The central zone of this kitchen-dining room is marked out by a coloured 'carpet' of terracotta, turquoise and olive green cement tiles that were manufactured for Emery & Cie according to traditional Moroccan techniques. As well as giving a colourful focus to the room, the hard-wearing tiles are a practical floor surface in heavy traffic areas. The clients often use a wax floor polisher after cleaning, which has resulted in the usually matte tiles taking on a rich glow.

RIGHT A bespoke sideboard was built to conceal a new staircase leading down to the basement. The wood used both for this and the kitchen table came from a school science laboratory, while the sliding door that fronts the sideboard was salvaged from the National Museum of Scotland. Instead of creating a solid, wall-like barrier between the kitchen and the staircase, the kitchen flooring (including a strip of tiles) runs beneath the raised base of the sideboard and onto the edge of the stairs, allowing the two spaces to flow seamlessly into one another. One side of the cupboard opens up to provide storage space for kitchen equipment; the other contains children's toys and books.

The wallpaper used in the entrance hall and along the main staircase is by designer-maker Daniel Heath, and was custom printed in milk chocolate tones for this project. Featuring images of birds in various stages of the taxidermy process, motifs from the wallpaper are repeated around the house in a variety of media. When developing his designs, Daniel Heath often visits the Natural History Museum in London for inspiration, so when Adam salvaged a batch of flat oak panels from the museum, it seemed a natural continuation to use them as the basis of a collaboration. One of the resulting laser-etched oak panels, featuring a bird design from the hallway wallpaper, has been inserted in the buttercup yellow wall of the basement of the house.

This idea of using aesthetic echoes to bring the spaces of a home together continues into the kitchen and dining room, where different materials merge into one another to create a sense of unity between the various areas. The floor combines reclaimed parquet with an inset section of patterned tiles. As well as being decorative, the tiles provide a tough, childproof floor surface

THIS PAGE AND OPPOSITE The lower ground floor of the house was extended on the garden side to create a summer dining room. Here again, a feature is made of the patterned cement-tile flooring, which extends beyond the folding doors right onto the garden terrace, so that on hot days, with the doors pulled back, the room becomes a part of the garden. Reclaimed stained-glass panels inlaid at irregular intervals lend the modern doors a sense of historical continuity and stop the more reserved contemporary architectural elements from appearing cold or intimidating. These coloured, patterned glass panels also draw the eye away from the plainer visible edges of the new extension, blurring its edges and focusing the eye on the longer view. A pair of Murano glass wall lights (above) give the sleek-edged space an injection of glamour.

LEFT In the relaxed living room of the lower ground floor, salvaged oak floorboards are run up the front of one wall, creating a sliding panel that conceals the television.

OPPOSITE The decorative panel set into the cupboard front at the bottom of the stairs is a reclaimed oak drawer bottom, laser-etched by Daniel Heath with one of the delicate bird motifs used in the custom-printed wallpaper that lines the hall staircase (see overleaf).

in those areas of the room that receive heaviest use. For similarly practical purposes, modern laminate doors were used on the wall-mounted kitchen units, but strips of reclaimed wood were run across them in horizontal and vertical lines to break up the plain surfaces and introduce a touch of colour. The horizontal strip was originally a set of drawer fronts, while the vertical one forms part of the fridge door. The laboratory origin of the

surfaces is given a playful nod in the use of old glass funnels for the lampshades above them.

The basement space combines an informal sitting room with a summer dining area that leads out onto the garden, and, indeed, virtually becomes a part of it once the folding doors are pulled back on warm days. The function of the rooms is kept flexible – a television is hidden behind a sliding panel in a wall-

THIS PAGE Much of the salvaged materials used in the house came from the National Museum of Scotland and their zoological origins have been picked up in the wallpaper created by Daniel Heath for the main stairwell, which features drawings of birds in the process of being stuffed for display.

mounted storage unit faced with the same reclaimed boards used for the floor, and a massive curtain made from one of the client's tweed designs can be drawn between the two rooms to cut the sitting room off and make it into a warmer den for winter, or a more formal daytime meeting space away from the hubbub of the kitchen and children.

As well as the family spaces pictured here, the home also contains an office and textile storage area in the basement. Clients often come to the house for meetings during the day, and their visit can be cut off from the main body of the home, as needed. "All the sliding doors and moving surfaces in the house have given it flexibility," explains the client. "I like the idea of living in a space all the time and keeping it flexible for working and entertaining and being with the kids. I don't separate my life into segments – I think of it all as parts of one life, and the house is the same; it reflects one continuous stream of living."

THIS PAGE The cupboards of this uplifting bathroom – one of the clients' favourite rooms – are faced in panels of heavily aged leather that was once used on shelves in The British Library. The warm, sunny aspect of the room is emphasized by the use of buttery yellow Zellige tiles and coordinating curtain fabric. The siding of the bathtub and the built-in shelves are made from the same hard-wearing salvaged hardwood as the kitchen surfaces.

MATERIAL PROFILE: LIGHTING

Lighting fixtures are the essential finishing details that give an interior expression and individuality. Well-chosen fittings make the difference between a space that feels like a token nod towards style and a room that constitutes a harmonious whole.

In a design based around salvaged components, the choice of lighting fixtures and anything electrical requires some thought; for any interior over a certain age, there is no such thing as a historically appropriate electrical light. The answer can be to adopt a different stylistic vocabulary altogether – many of the Victorian houses in this book feature mid-century lighting fixtures, for example. Salvaged lights and lamps should always be rewired by a qualified electrician before installation, and any appliance intended to be used in a bathroom must be adapted for use in a damp environment. The quality of light can be as important a factor as the fixture itself – for older homes, Maria tends to use high-quality filament bulbs, which give a warmer, softer light.

THIS PAGE AND OPPOSITE Making functional objects such as light fittings do some of the decorative work can stop an interior becoming too cluttered. Thoughtful details such as the braided textile-sleeved cable used to rewire these lampshades (right) really count when adapting salvaged pieces for an interior.
ABOVE RIGHT Found in a junk shop, this wall lamp is one of Adam and Maria's favourite pieces, and takes pride of place in their kitchen.

RIGHT AND OPPOSITE With both parents working from different spaces within this home plus busy teenage children, the long kitchen-dining room is an important social hub for family, colleagues and friends. The building's industrial past is referenced by the factory lights, but the room is softened by the inclusion of sofas and a large Berber rug between the kitchen and the dining table.

This unique family home pulls together a Georgian terraced house and a converted Victorian factory building to create an exciting and hard-working modern living space. Already strongly committed to using salvaged materials, the owners approached Retrouvius to adapt the home to their evolving needs.

FORMER FACTORY

Walking up to the classical front door of the Georgian Grade II listed house that forms the exterior face of this property, one wouldn't for a moment imagine the sweeping former industrial space that lies at the heart of this home. Stepping through the entrance hall, you are drawn towards a long, glass-ceilinged kitchen-dining room decorated with antique crockery and factory lanterns. The room is the congregation point for the family, offering sofas to lounge on, a dining table, an open kitchen area and a concealed larder.

The original conversion of the building took place in 2005, under the eye of architect Charles Tashima. The main house, dating from the 1760s, was abutted by a former Victorian factory space; the roof was corrugated plastic and the basement was open to bare earth. The conversion was an enormous undertaking and was conducted with a strong emphasis on reclaimed materials at every stage. The clients

THIS PAGE AND OPPOSITE
This larder space is hidden behind the stove unit shown in the photograph on page 40. It allows the kitchen to remain essentially open plan but the functional aspects of kitchen work to happen out of sight of guests. The leather panels facing the units came from The British Library. The wooden storage vessels incorporated within some of the units were already in the clients' collection.

first encountered Retrouvius when purchasing stock from the warehouse, including the flooring, wood for the kitchen surfaces and the handsome closet doors in the master bedroom.

The clients chose to use reclaimed materials out of respect for old and well-made things, and to keep the building true to its history. "The idea of the building was not to slavishly reproduce how it might have been with a Georgian front and Victorian back, but to be true to the building itself," explains the client. "It has lines and bumps, and gravity has had its way. Rather than give it a facelift, we wanted to restore it to its own beauty."

Maria was brought in as a designer at a later stage, a few years after the conversion had been completed, when the family's needs changed as their children grew older. Since an architectural language had already been established, the key was to work with

THIS PAGE AND OPPOSITE These clients have a very serious commitment to salvage and reuse. Long before Maria worked on any design aspect of this home, they were clients of Adam's, and visited the warehouse during the original renovation of the building for salvaged materials. Much of the flooring and wood used in the house comes from Adam, and one of Retrouvius's regular joiners worked with the original architect, Charles Tashima, to create the kitchen. Adam also supplied major pieces, such as these folding doors (opposite, above left) forming the wardrobe front in the master bedroom. Original industrial features from the old building are still visible above them. The mid-century furniture used in the master bedroom (left) works happily alongside the Georgian architecture because the arrangement has been kept simple – the pieces have space to dictate their own aesthetic within the room. Behind the wardrobe, the master bathroom created by the clients (opposite, far right and below left) features salvaged floorboards cladding the wall above the basin, a cabinet topped in reclaimed hardwood, a free-standing bathtub and a panel of handmade tiles behind the bath taps.

that and to extend the aesthetic to adapt to the family's evolving lifestyle. "Maria has big things to say about how people live their lives," recalls the client. "She talked to us about how we live, where we gather, when we separate, who went where with whom and how we fit together. She guarded us against being unrealistic about our behaviour. A lot of architects are all about form – Maria is interested in form and function, but also in behaviour."

Small adjustments were made to the main kitchen and dining area to make it more friendly and relaxing – both parents work from home, so the kitchen is a place for the family to regroup and switch off. The informality of the space was emphasized by the choice of comfortable old chairs and a made-to-measure dining table topped with reclaimed hardwood. Sofas were placed between the kitchen and the dining table, so that one parent could cook and the other could relax in the same space.

The client had always wanted a larder but had run out of both time and energy to create one during the first phase of the building project. Maria knocked through a room at the back of

the kitchen to create a space that provided practical, functional storage and additional workspace. Cupboards were faced with old leather salvaged from the British Library and new storage was created under the surfaces using antique containers already owned by the clients.

Upstairs, within the Georgian part of the house, Maria created a more grown-up bedroom layout for one of the children, and a new guest bedroom, the design of which is centred around a piece of vibrant yellow fabric that the clients had brought back from India. The guest bedroom is small, but fits in plenty of storage, including drawers featuring mahogany fronts taken from the

THIS PAGE In one of the children's bedrooms (left), a desk and shelving unit was built using oak salvaged from a school (below). In a typical Maria touch, the oak panelling from the drawer fronts has been continued up the wall to create the backdrop to miniature shelves, and the lines of the handles are echoed in another set of tiny shelves at the side. The lines and angles of the piece become abstract and decorative as well as functional.

National Museum of Scotland in Edinburgh. Adam recalls that around 2000 drawer fronts were removed during a renovation at the museum, but that they had all been built in, so had no sides. From most practical perspectives they were just valueless pieces of wood, but with a little imagination, and thanks to the quality of the materials, their history and patina make them into something special. This little guest bedroom is full of elements that are both practical and decorative. "She made a tiny room feel like a world of its own," says the client. "Maria gives as much importance to the corner as to the main stage. It's not a part of many people's practice."

Beneath the long, glass-ceilinged kitchen, the basement of the old factory had been given over to the clients' extensive library. The function of the

THIS PAGE The adjacent bathroom was redecorated using tongue-and-groove panelling taken from a large church hall, different sections of which had been painted in various colours and finishes. It was reassembled with the sections in random order, which created a patchwork effect. The panelling was used to clad both the lower part of the bathroom wall and the high cupboard doors that run along one side of it.

THIS PAGE AND OPPOSITE With both relatives and work colleagues often staying, the guest bedroom has to fulfil multiple functions. It needs to be comfortable enough for extended visits, with all the wardrobe space that entails, and to offer space to work and watch DVDs. All the storage, the desk and television are stacked in a tall cupboard (opposite below right) which has drawers faced in salvaged drawer fronts from a museum. The headboard of the bed (this page) was upholstered in Indian fabric that was already owned by the clients and the reverse side of a salvaged textile panel originally destined for use on bus seats. The vibrant yellow of the Indian fabric has been picked up in cushions and in the upholstery of the armchair (opposite, above right).

room morphs depending on the parents' work requirements and on what the children are up to. Before Maria redesigned the space it had been more functional, used partly as an editing suite and partly as a viewing room. There was no staircase to access the room properly and there were bookshelves running all around the outside wall. In developing a space like this, Maria explains that finding the right design is often a question of looking at the materials that already exist within the room, and then finding more of them, so that the space retains its own spirit. "There was already tongue-and-groove panelling and oak shelving," she explains. Using more of the existing materials respects the personality of the space. The flooring and the additional panelling on the walls were all made using reclaimed wood.

THIS PAGE AND OPPOSITE
In the basement library, Maria wanted to retain the existing atmosphere and texture of the original materials. There was already some old tongue-and-groove panelling on the walls, so she brought in more and used it across the front of the cabinets that run along the side of the new staircase. Paint sits differently on old wood, so there is a logic to using reclaimed materials, even when their presence isn't glaringly obvious.

Maria wanted to break up the huge space to allow for more books but without using solid shelving. She installed adjustable cast-iron shelving units that had been salvaged from the Patent Office in Chancery Lane, central London. The units are free standing, and double sided, but without a solid back to the shelves they don't look too heavy. By bringing in sofas and other pieces from elsewhere in the house, she created areas of intimacy and cosiness that now allow the library to be used more as an evening drawing room rather than as a workspace.

While the emphasis on salvage at the heart of this home stems from a deep-rooted respect for fine materials and for functional, well-used pieces, it has almost accidentally also ended up creating the dominant aesthetic. Rather than being centred on artworks and purely decorative elements, the style of this home is dominated by rich textures, generous spaces and beautifully aged materials that give it great spirit, and warmth, while allowing it to remain resolutely practical.

GARDEN CABIN

Set off a busy intersection in central London, the fairytale rusticity of this garden cabin is a most unexpected treat. Opening up along its full front with a set of four salvaged folding door panels that give out onto a little private deck, it's a comfortable and private space that in fine weather can be opened up to the fresh air, but in winter provides a warm, well-insulated retreat.

Planning permission had been obtained by a previous owner for a small building at the bottom of his garden. The cabin that was eventually built by Retrouvius shares almost identical proportions to the boxy structure depicted in the planning application, but it could not be more different in spirit.

The client, a debonair man-about-town, wanted a very evident salvage style for the cabin, which gives it an immediately informal, lived-in atmosphere. It is, however, a completely 'new' building, which not only allows for a certain degree of modern comfort to be written into the design but also means that the proportions of the cabin could be tailor-made to maximize the use of salvaged materials. The sliding doors along the front were originally

THIS PAGE AND OPPOSITE
The same batch of hardwood floorboards was used both inside the cabin and on the deck in front, which creates a feeling of connection with the garden and extends the floor space on warm days, when the sliding doors can be left open. The 'bridge' (above) was added at a later date, during a redesign of the garden. It was constructed from similar materials and looks wonderful with the worn timber of the deck.

chapel partitions from Herefordshire, and still show their original paintwork. They were already designed to fold and slide, but were refitted to run on modern tracks. Because the cabin and everything in it was created from scratch, the size of the front could be adjusted to make it a perfect fit for the size of the doors. Likewise, the dimensions of the small shower room were dictated by the size of some salvaged panels of Derbyshire fossil limestone. A commitment to reusing materials also involves thinking about the ongoing life of a material, and what might happen to it once it is removed from its current context. It is always preferable to leave materials like this uncut or unaltered in order to increase their potential for reuse.

The interior of the cabin has a surprising jauntiness and is dominated by a palette of three materials: the limestone, hardwood flooring taken from a school, and tongue-and-groove panelling that had originally been painted in

ABOVE LEFT AND RIGHT A painted wood partition from a chapel was reinvented as a sliding door that runs across the front of the cabin.
OPPOSITE Tongue-and-groove-panelling has been interspersed with floorboards and laid horizontally along the walls. Installing panels or boards in this way is like a jigsaw puzzle in which the arrangement of the pieces is dictated only by considerations of size. The random patchwork patterns and mismatching colours that are generated by this process bring an aesthetic dimension of their own. The shelves that run along the side of the bed are made of old pew seats set on ornate cast-iron brackets.

THIS PAGE Dark hardwood floorboards line one wall of the cabin in two vertical blocks on either side of a limestone panel. On the left, the panel of boards forms the face of the bathroom door. It is echoed in size and shape by a panel to the right that conceals a hanging cupboard.

three different colours. Beneath the salvaged cladding, the cabin is heavily insulated throughout, which meant that the job of heating the space could be left to two modern trench radiators that are concealed beneath a pair of old church grilles. As an alternative light source, three Velux windows were set into the roof and the exterior turrets were clad in reclaimed timber.

Rather than having the doors of the cabin expensively double-glazed, they were hung with thick curtains made of antique patchwork backed with new linen to block out the cold in the winter. A similar set of curtains was also hung in the bedroom of the main house – not only do they keep the space warm but they also act as a stylish alternative to blackout curtains.

THIS PAGE Salvaged fittings have been used throughout the cabin, including a fabulous old showerhead and an enchanting little pedestal handbasin that has been plumbed into the bedroom wall (above), as well as vintage lamps, and mirrors. A love of salvaged items led the client to source these old metal wall hooks (above right), which now hang by the cabin door.

While the cabin is now perhaps the most arresting aspect of this project, it was, in truth, something of an afterthought to the work carried out in the main house. Set at the end of a stucco-fronted Victorian terrace in North London, the two-storey apartment occupies the raised ground floor and a garden-level basement. Before Retrouvius's involvement, the property had already been converted, with the upper floor opened out into an open-plan living space, and the basement used for bedrooms and bathrooms. Although the apartment was filled with light and space, the client felt it lacked both individuality and ease.

In a quest to inject some of his personal style into the space, he started hunting for objects and textiles to dress it with. His search took him to the

Retrouvius warehouse, and the moment he walked in, he experienced a kind of love at first sight. "I loved the vibe of the place," he recalls. "I wanted my whole flat to feel like that." He graduated from buying some pieces from the warehouse to meeting Maria – who he now describes as a "friend and mentor" – and deciding that she was the perfect person to steer the interior of his home in the right direction.

LEFT This large pink cupboard was salvaged from a Protestant church, where it had once been used to store clerical vestments. It sits along one wall of the kitchen and serves as an informal pinboard as well as a storage unit.

THIS PAGE AND OPPOSITE, RIGHT The variegated shell pink hues of these Zellige tiles was perhaps an unusual choice for a bachelor flat, but they provide an interestingly soft counterbalance to the scuffed, mismatched and often quasi-industrial salvaged furniture.

Perhaps the most significant intervention in the space was a whole wall of pink Zellige tiles, which, as the client notes, is quite a bold move in a bachelor flat. Zellige tiles are handmade in Morocco and are by their nature inconsistent in colour, so the result is a wave of softly variegated plaster pink hues. Tiling all the way up to the ceiling pulls the space together and the colour gives it a soft warmth that relaxes the space. It also brings some unity to the jumble of surfaces and storage units that make up the unfitted kitchen.

Quite a quantity of textiles was brought into the apartment to make it feel more relaxed – cushions faced with salvaged fabric, an old sofa with its original blue silk upholstery and thick patchwork for the master bedroom. Interesting storage pieces were installed, including a set of old pâtisserie shelves in the downstairs study and a number of pew backs stacked one on top of the other beside the front door, which create shelves for keys and cards. "You can have all these composite parts, but there's no cohesion to them," recalls the client. "She just pulled the whole place together. All of a sudden it didn't feel like some weird mishmash – it felt like there was a design to it."

OPPOSITE Opposite the front door a set of little shelves for invitations, keys and other oddments was created out of a quantity of bible rests stacked one on top of one another up the wall. They were originally set into the back of church pews.
ABOVE The client had a particular affection for keeping objects in their found state, such as this old sofa that still has its original blue silk upholstery, which gives his home a relaxed vibe.
RIGHT AND FAR RIGHT This adjustable shelving allows for the display not only of books but also works of art and objects. Arranged like this, it prevents the television from becoming the central focus of the multi-purpose living space.

Hardwood is a very precious natural resource, and many of the tropical hardwoods salvaged by Retrouvius are no longer available from sustainable sources. This is one area in which salvage is less a stylistic choice than an ethical imperative.

MATERIAL PROFILE: WOOD

OPPOSITE AND BELOW Heavily used strips of parquet (opposite) taken from a school gymnasium tend to be uneven and worn down in patches from years of use. To be reinstalled as flooring, they need to be put through a belt sander to flatten the surface before polishing. To create a textured wall cladding, such as the one shown in the Barbican project (below and on pages 16–25), the pieces must be sanded individually.

RIGHT AND FAR RIGHT Iroko surfaces from school science laboratories (far right) arrive in the warehouse looking unappetizing, bearing years of graffiti and chewed gum. Sanded and treated, the beautiful colour and grain of the wood are apparent in the worksurfaces and tabletop of this kitchen (right), and in the wooden frame around the cooker.

Of all the used materials that come into the warehouse, wood has perhaps the least evident appeal but, treated right, it has yielded some of the most spectacular effects. "If you look at a hardwood floor that's been lifted, it will be splintery; it will have old varnish and dirt and probably the old nails in it," explains Adam. "Anyone who doesn't know will look at a pile of reclaimed wood and think it's a bonfire. But it's two tonnes of teak that's still usable. Yes, you have to take the nails out; yes, you have to sand it back; yes, you have to revarnish it and handle it in a certain way. It all sounds so obvious now, but I think people used to think that it was more trouble than it was worth and would just go and buy new stuff."

LAKESIDE HOUSE

After three moves in seven years, this family most recently set up home in the crisp mountain air of a pretty Swiss country town. As keen collectors, one of the most pressing questions was how to adapt the furniture from their previous homes in London and Berlin to their very different new residence.

These clients joke that Maria is famous in their family for her compulsion to move furniture around, often late into the night. With a deeply ingrained dislike of waste of any kind, she is always determined to make existing furniture function harmoniously in a new setting. It's a compulsion – and indeed talent – that first came into play for them seven years ago, when the now husband and wife moved in together.

What was to become their first family home originally belonged to the husband and was filled with his furniture collection, dominated by sturdy wooden pieces such as aeroplane propellers and heavy

THIS PAGE AND OPPOSITE Both husband and wife are keen cooks, and knew that this kitchen and dining room was going to be the heart of the home. The design needed to accommodate both the needs of hordes of sticky-fingered children and adults engaged in rather more civilized dinner parties later in the evening. One very simple solution was to provide two sets of seating – a rather smart set of 1940s Italian chairs that the client found in Berlin to be used by the grown-ups, and a pair of benches covered in salvaged red leather for the children, which can be stashed against the wall when not in use.

LEFT AND OPPOSITE The oak drawer and cupboard fronts in this kitchen were originally a set of four fluted pilasters from a church in Marylebone, central London. Usually pilasters are tapered, but this set was straight, which meant that they could be used horizontally, stacked one above the other in parallel. This is a very long kitchen, so took six metres (20 feet) of cupboards, drawers and worksurfaces. The fluted fronts of the pilasters actually accentuate that length and make the most of it. The worksurface is a heavily battered and graffitied piece of hardwood that was originally a school laboratory top.

refectory tables. When the couple decided to live together, not only did the décor feel overwhelmingly masculine but there also seemed to be very little space for another person with their own very distinctive taste to settle in. Maria came in to reconcile the two distinct personalities within the house, and to make out of it a space in which both husband and wife felt at home.

The clients and their two young children next moved from London to Berlin, where they took full advantage of the wonderful vintage stores in the city, accumulating even more furniture before moving to a large house in a small town in Switzerland. The late nineteenth-century building had previously been the residency of the British Ambassador, and was in good

LEFT AND BELOW This wooden parquet flooring was hidden beneath an alarming orange-tinged 1970s varnish. Stripped and stained, it now looks immensely elegant and complements the fine vintage furniture.

OPPOSITE Back in the 1970s, the house had been redesigned for the British Ambassador and thus it has a huge reception room for formal entertaining. The room's generous proportions means that it is able to accommodate large and eye-catching pieces of furniture, such as this unusual lacquered wardrobe that the owners brought with them from their previous home. With shelves installed, it becomes a practical piece of storage for the drawing room, and hides the family's television set. Each time this family moves house, Maria spends ages moving their furniture around into different positions to see where it will look best – with the result that the same set of furniture ends up transformed each time.

condition. Maria was initially asked to create a kitchen better suited to the needs of a busy family. Both husband and wife were keen cooks and knew that the kitchen would end up being the space in which the family congregated. They wanted a large, well-equipped kitchen, fitted in old materials, that somehow felt as though it had always been in the house.

Maria tried hunting through some salvage yards in Switzerland for materials to use in the kitchen, but they turned out to be so expensive that it was more cost-effective to source the materials in Britain. The fronts and surfaces use a combination of oak pilasters – salvaged by Adam from a church in London – and Iroko laboratory tops, but the internal workings of all the units are new,

OPPOSITE Maria and the client went through a great bundle of curtains from previous homes, working out which ones might work where, then they chose the paint colours to match the curtains, rather than vice versa. This lavender blue set had previously hung in the family's home in Berlin, and were cut down to fit the windows in the Swiss home.

LEFT AND BELOW After working with Maria on her homes, this client says that she has picked up a very particular sensibility of how a home should fit together. "I really wanted each room to be an extension of the room before, so that every room looked good from the doorway of the next."

and the effect of a well-loved old kitchen was created with relatively little material. All the wood was kept in its rough state to retain as much texture and personality as possible, and the refrigerator and freezer were given copper doors and salvaged handles to stop them looking jarringly new. The wall behind them was covered in greeny-grey tiles that look gorgeous against the copper.

The room was completed with a simple polished concrete floor that echoed the grey of the tiles, and the addition of a new picture window that allowed the family to look out over the beautiful Swiss landscape. Maria also designed some benches, covered in red leather salvaged from the luxury brand Dunhill, which had apparently been destined for a custom car interior.

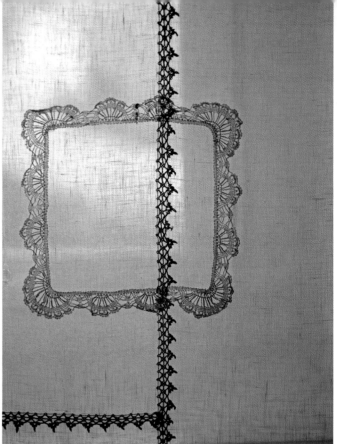

THIS PAGE AND OPPOSITE Delicate nets diffuse the sunlight in this bathroom. The blind (above and opposite) was made by London-based designer Lucy Bathurst, who regularly collaborates with Retrouvius. It features salvaged scraps of handmade lace backed with cotton voile and arranged to create a decorative geometric pattern. Pieces of fabric can often be found in a deteriorated condition that renders them too delicate to be used in their existing state. Reinforced by natural contemporary fabrics, they can be enjoyed without being damaged. While protected from direct sunlight by the voile backing, the light from the window brings out the lovely detail in the lace.

Having worked with Maria and observed her style over the years, some of the clients' collection had been accumulated under her influence, including vintage Berber rugs from Larusi. Back in London they had also admired a magnificent Lurçat tapestry that she had in her home (see page 128), and have since picked up a number of similarly bold twentieth-century designs.

Maria worked with them to position the tapestries and rugs in the new house, using these as the departure point from which to select paint colours and fabrics that would pull the rooms

together. "She doesn't cut corners," explains the client. " For Maria, it's all in the details. She'll spend hours going through the correct details to finish things off with." It took Maria four complete rearrangements to get the furniture into a position that she felt happy with, but the result is an excellent lesson in how, with the use of interesting fabrics, detailed fittings, well-selected paint colours and an inventive eye for positioning, it is possible to move between very different styles of house with the same collection of furniture and make it work beautifully in each one.

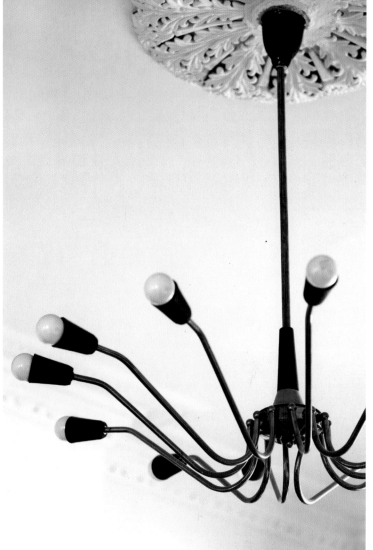

OPPOSITE AND ABOVE The front fireplace is surrounded by a thick band of wonderful glossy brown tiles, reminiscent of the shiny brown paper in a smart box of chocolates. They introduce an edge of glamour into a scheme that is otherwise quite restrained. Certainly, they are in dramatic contrast to the rough texture and monolithic outline of the cast concrete bench that runs across the front of the fireplace.

ABOVE Many 1950s pieces were used, including reconditioned wall and ceiling lamps, a beautifully decorative cocktail cabinet that the client uses to store sheet music and a chair and sofa that were upholstered in complementary tones to bring a sense of continuity to the space. Bringing 1950s shapes into a Victorian terraced house like this works perfectly, so long as there is space for them to 'breathe'.

CITY TERRACE

When sharing a house with young children, it's easy to get so caught up in the day-to-day that you forget the quieter, less frenetic moments that a family can enjoy together. This project was all about creating a living space that was at once culturally fulfilling for the parents and perfect for relaxed Sunday afternoons *en famille*.

OPPOSITE The concrete bench that runs along the chimneybreast wall plays a triple role, providing storage space for logs and boxes containing children's toys, as well as additional seating. The boxes that hold the children's toys come from a factory in Cheshire that used to make children's ballet shoes for the famous Gandolfi dance shop in London.

LEFT AND BELOW The starting points for the décor in these rooms were two beautiful Callum Innes paintings owned by the clients. The tonal colour palette of these paintings provided a base set of stony colours that were used in the rugs, the floorboards and the upholstery. Touches of buttercup yellow were introduced to brighten the space.

With all the bustle of family life, the living room on the ground floor of this home had gradually turned into a dumping ground for overspill from the hallway, cluttered with buggies and scooters. The basement kitchen had become the heart of the home by default, and the clients were desperate for a comfortable room where they could play and listen to music, or hang out with their children.

The first stage in the transformation was to create a storage space in the front garden to accommodate scooters, bicycles and prams. This allowed the living room to be returned to its original function. At some stage, a wall had been removed between what were originally two separate rooms to create a single space. As a result, the conjoined room had two doorways to the hall. One door was replaced with a large pane of glass, which allows light to flow into the hallway from the windows at the back of the room, and gives anyone entering an inviting view of the garden.

THIS PAGE AND OPPOSITE, ABOVE LEFT
The Modernist proportions of the Callum
Innes paintings (see previous pages) are
echoed in the design of this chimneybreast.
Rather than giving space to another
artwork, the tiled surface is broken up by
a mirror and two slim strips of metal that
continue the perpendicular lines formed by
the two axes of the fireplace itself.

Because there are so few pieces of furniture in the room, each one has to act almost as a piece of sculpture, so it needed crisp shapes full of personality; not squashy country-style sofas. It's a kind of luscious minimalism; the space looks very elegant so long as it's not cluttered. When considering an interior such as this, it is important to be realistic about the way you will live in it. We often have ambitions for our space that we can't achieve because it doesn't fit realistically with our lifestyles or personalities.

ABOVE RIGHT AND RIGHT
To prevent anyone from walking into this glass panel, four decorative gilded dividers salvaged from a church were positioned in front of it. They create a beautiful focal point in the hallway (right) leading the eye to the back reception room and the garden beyond.

THIS PAGE AND OPPOSITE The three batches of stone seen installed on this page were salvaged from a stonemason's yard (far left), Heathrow's Terminal 2 (left) and a corporate lobby (below). They are all limited materials – the tiny stock of gilded marble and fireplace roundels (below and far left) was all used up in the kitchen of one home (see page 108). The fossil limestone salvaged from Heathrow features in many of the projects in this book because it was part of the warehouse's stock at that time. Supplies of the stone have since run out; with salvaged materials there is a thrill in knowing that you are using something rare, but this brings the responsibility of treating it with respect.

Like wood, stone is a limited – and hard-won – natural resource. It has a very distinctive geographical personality, and much of the stock that Retrouvius salvages is identifiable right down to its particular quarry, like the Derbyshire fossil limestone that Adam removed from Heathrow's Terminal 2 building.

MATERIAL PROFILE: STONE

It was actually the response to their first big batch of salvaged stone – green Westmorland slate taken from the façade of a building in Blackfriars – that taught Maria how resistant many architects were to working with salvaged materials. They were so nervous about their liability in specifying a less predictable, less standardized material that the architects would suggest that their clients bypass them, buy it directly and instruct the builders themselves. Stone flooring that has been heavily worn certainly brings its own problems in reuse: decades of footfall can wear stone down and create variations in thickness that mean it demands great care when it is relaid, even as cladding on a wall. Retrouvius collaborate very closely with builders so that they can all deal with and learn from any problems raised by each new batch of materials.

MEDIEVAL PRIORY

This ancient priory building had been well looked after and sensitively restored. The task for Retrouvius was to transform it into a comfortable weekend house for a lively modern family, without losing touch with its aesthetic roots.

OPPOSITE AND ABOVE RIGHT
"It sounds ludicrous," says the client, "but our kitchen was so uncomfortable. Then Maria turned the table around, and the whole experience of being in the room was transformed. Turning the table made way for a sofa and chair – it's so comfortable"
ABOVE LEFT The ground floor is floored in Suffolk pamments – clay floor tiles traditionally used in the East of England.

Old English country houses have a reputation for being immensely uncomfortable. The prospect of a stay in a sixteenth-century house conjures up images of draughty rooms, lumpy furniture, skull-crushingly low beams and erratic plumbing. Attempts to impose modern decorative ideas on old spaces often look awkward – straight lines and hard corners can argue with the irregular, age-settled curves of an ancient building.

When working with an old building like this one, it can be difficult to find the right balance between letting the age and architecture of the house dictate every design choice, and creating a practical family home. The knack is

ABOVE AND ABOVE LEFT
Retrouvius sourced this fragment of fragile eighteenth-century crewel work. There was just enough of it to be used in the design of the natural linen blind that hangs in the kitchen.

to be sympathetic to the language of the building without being overly pedantic about it. The welcoming, comfortable spaces created by Retrouvius in this Suffolk home are the result not only of stylistic sensitivity and well-sourced materials but a deep affection for and intellectual engagement with ancient buildings.

For Maria, a childhood visit to William Morris's country house, Kelmscott Manor, turned out to be a formative experience. "I remember it as being extraordinarily beautiful," she explains. "It had a huge influence on me, particularly in the way that these very early vernacular buildings incorporated textiles. Georgian buildings are full of flat planes for displaying art, but in these ancient buildings, textiles become the artwork. In ancient buildings, the functional spaces are where you create beauty."

William Morris described Kelmscott as looking as though it had "grown up out of the soil", so naturally did it seem to emerge from its setting. Although not as grand as Kelmscott, this Suffolk farmhouse dates from about the same period and likewise features a rich palette of local materials from the time of its construction, including clay floor tiles and heavy timbers. Formerly the property of the Society for the Protection of Ancient Buildings (an organization, coincidentally, co-founded by

OPPOSITE AND BELOW In the downstairs sitting room, this curtain was originally created by Kirsten Hecktermann for a group show that Retrouvius held at their warehouse to showcase the work of some of the designers that they regularly collaborate with.

Kirsten created a vast banner patchworked with hand-dyed velvet, vintage linen, lace and crochet work. The banner was reinvented as a curtain for this house.
RIGHT Retrouvius found this magnificent Italian *cassone* (marriage chest) for the house.

William Morris himself), the house had never been tampered with and any repairs had been carried out in accordance with very strict conservation practice.

While this meant that no actual building work should – or could – take place, it also meant that every scrap of furniture (including kitchen and bathroom units) had to be unfitted, and that the only way to modify the space and bring personality and attitude in was through the creative use of textiles. Irrespective of the need to protect the fabric of the building itself, this ethos fitted well with the aesthetic of the home – there was not a straight line or right angle to be found anywhere within the structure, so it seemed to openly invite the fluid fit of textiles and correspondingly asymmetrical old furnishings.

The first task was to take the building right back to its intrinsic aesthetic – removing the fitted carpets and allowing the exposed timbers to dictate the language of the interior. Maria describes her approach as sticking to the spirit of the building rather than doggedly paying obeisance to the actual age of the structure.

LEFT AND OPPOSITE The embroidered panels used on these cushions are very fine Spanish work from the late eighteenth century that would have been quite valuable had they been in better condition. Many of the textile pieces that Kirsten sources are too far gone to be purchased for a museum collection. She uses scraps of them in her work, backed with a stronger base textile such as linen, and quite often they will become the basis for the design of a whole room. To Kirsten, part of the charm of such pieces is that they do deteriorate.

In outfitting the home, she searched for objects that had "the requisite degree of wonkiness", be they a Hungarian dresser, French tapestry fragments, Moroccan shawls or Dutch linens. It didn't matter where or when precisely they came from, the pieces had to have "the right vernacular" – those things that were not ancient or salvaged had a handmade or natural element to them that allowed them to feel at home. Having removed the carpets, she put handmade rugs over the exposed timbers on the upper floor and the traditional pamments on the lower floors, and laid down natural woven jute in the attic.

"It was about trying to find the right pieces to fit in that had an older look but were also comfortable," Maria explains. "We

looked for early rush seats, but chose very comfortable sofas and beds. We went for simple modern pieces, such as Van Duysen sofas, that work well in both old and new houses." Maria is also always careful not to select furniture for a single position within a home – she finds pieces that work well with the spirit of the house as a whole rather than a particular room. This allows spaces to evolve over time.

Working with salvage is not all slabs of slate and chunks of rare hardwood; it's also about cherishing the beauty of special things by creating a sympathetic new context for them. Old textiles and embroidered panels bring a soft, hand-worked quality into a room, and their aged colours can be taken as the

THIS PAGE AND OPPOSITE It is not easy to source practical lamps that would look at home in an ancient building like this one. In many of the rooms, Maria ended up creating table lights out of old glass bottles, soda siphons and demijohns, and topping them with very simple lampshades. The old glass was unobtrusive and had the requisite wonkiness to it. Although the building had been very well preserved, Maria changed many of the existing fittings to make the lighting softer and less intense, and more appropriate for the rooms.

basis for a whole decorative palette. This can be particularly effective when selecting a colour scheme for an old house that has distinctive architectural features and a very particular quality of light. By bringing a selection of salvaged textiles into the space at the start of the design process, you can assess what might work best for the room and the personalities that will inhabit it. By gently patching them together with contemporary fabrics, delicate old pieces of lacework and embroidery that would otherwise be too fragile to use can become the centrepiece of a room. All the bedspreads and curtains were made for the house using salvaged textiles, which allowed them to integrate the modern pieces into the old building.

For much of the textile work in this project, Retrouvius worked with regular collaborator Kirsten Hecktermann, a former costume designer who now specializes in salvaging scraps of exquisite old materials that are too deteriorated to be of interest to museums. From her

THIS PAGE AND OPPOSITE The house had been very well preserved and sympathetically repaired under very strict conservation practice by the Society for the Protection of Ancient Buildings but prior to the renovation had been fitted with carpets in eye-watering royal blue and a shade that Maria describes as "pub carpet red". She wanted to tone everything down, and to allow the exposed timbers of the building to dictate the aesthetic of the interior. In many rooms, complementary curtains and upholstery were made from good old natural linen – a mixture of Hungarian, Dutch and French – that had the right texture and weight.

experience in creating period costumes for films, Kirsten learned how to hand dye fabric (she says that the first job that involved her employing this technique was Zeffirelli's *Hamlet* with Mel Gibson). It's a skill that she has brought with her into her new career; for this home, she hand dyed velvets and linens to be used as upholstery fabric on armchairs and sofas. Because the fabric is dyed multiple times, the effect is subtle, giving the upholstery a luxurious richness that looks as though it has developed over time.

Large cushions were used as a key feature of the house, bringing comfort into the space and creating islands of softness and colour within rooms. The less-heavily used of these feature embroidery salvaged by Kirsten. "When I first started to make cushions, I worried that they would fall apart if they weren't

ABOVE AND RIGHT Scraps of salvaged textiles were the
starting point for many schemes – in this case, the
eighteenth-century crewelwork panel on the bedcover
was the inspiration, and its blue shades are echoed in
the chair upholstery and a Welsh blanket.
OPPOSITE Because the fabric of the building could
not be touched, this project saw Maria using textiles
architecturally rather than just decoratively. This heavy
curtain features a panel taken from an embroidered
shawl. It brings not only beauty and brightness into the
home but also introduces privacy and warmth; in a
building where you could not install a door, this screen
does the job in its stead.

just used for decoration," she says. "But cushions have to be
functional, and part of the charm is that they do disintegrate –
it gives them a bit of an age. If you do a whole house in new
things, it looks too sterile. The occupants of any house will pick
up and add to things over time – it helps the whole feel of a
house to have different time zones in it."

To strengthen the aged lace and embroidery pieces, Kirsten
sews them by hand onto a stronger base fabric and catches them
down securely in any areas where they are looking weak. It was
this desire to give new life to beautiful old pieces that were

disintegrating that brought her to work with salvaged fabric in
the first place, and she feels that she and Maria share a common
sensibility in their desire to reinvent and reuse things but above
all keep them functional.

While using as much salvaged material as possible in the
design, Maria was also concerned not to make the interior too
much of a museum piece. "There is a simplicity that you get in
vernacular architecture that can be incredibly modern," she
explains. "I didn't want it to look too fusty." Although every single
piece in the interior had to be brought in, she worked towards

ABOVE LEFT AND RIGHT, AND OPPOSITE With a tiny, narrow staircase, it was impossible to get substantial pieces of furniture into the upper floors of the house in one piece. Many of the beds were made in situ. Other things had to be adapted – taken apart before they were brought into the house, then put back together again. The necessity of such efforts meant that it wasn't an appropriate home for incredibly precious or rare antiques. Most of the furniture is a mix of salvaged oddments and simple modern pieces toned down with clever upholstery.

LEFT These little glass pendant lamps above the bed are actually running out of a nearby plug socket. Nothing more substantial than a screw to hold up the cast-iron coat hook they hang from has been inserted into the beams.

creating a decorative portrait of a family that had lived in the house over many centuries, adding to it progressively as time went by. This home is intended to look as though it has evolved over generations, rather than sprung untouched through a 500-year time warp.

Because of the tiny staircase and wobbly angles of the home, many of the larger pieces had to taken apart and rebuilt in situ (Maria refers to the process they had to go through as "Medieval flat-pack"). Others, such as the ottoman with a cast iron base in the sitting room (see page 86), were pieced together from a mixture of salvaged and new materials. The task of outfitting the house was simplified by the fact that this wasn't the clients' primary residence – rather than having to deal with the existing clutter of a family and provide huge amounts of storage space and wardrobes, Maria could concentrate on simply providing what they needed for a comfortable week away.

The central role that textiles play in the interior has been a revelation for the client. "Maria encouraged us to leave the house alone, but to have many more curtains and cushions and soft things," she recalls. "She said that we could let the house be gracefully decrepit if there were things for human beings to sit down on and cuddle into.

It's a lovely experience to be there, because you always know where to be in every room."

The client's interest in a salvaged style sprang from a fascination with ancient objects and the way that, in earlier periods, it was often the most useful things that received the most decorative attention. "I've always loved what went before – I'm not so keen on current fashion. I feel passionately for how things work; functional forms," she explains. "That doesn't mean that everything should be ugly – people have always beautified functional objects. In the British Museum you can see how people have decorated old pots. I've been reusing old things in contemporary settings for about thirty years – I'm almost upset that fashion has caught up with me!"

THIS PAGE AND OPPOSITE This beautifully restored nineteenth-century fairground traveller's caravan in the garden is a perfect secret hideout for a quiet afternoon with a book. The traditional burgundy paintwork of the exterior has been perfectly picked up in the vintage Welsh blanket on the raised bed, which in turn provided the green colour used to paint the woodwork of the interior.

These clients' previous home had been an apartment with Art Deco proportions. In bringing decorative elements to their new home, some work was necessary to adapt them to suit the dimensions of a Victorian terraced house. A pair of Klimt-esque Neisha Crosland curtains were reused as decorative panels on a new, wider pair of curtains in the sitting room of the new home (opposite). The ex-London museum Victorian furniture (right) sourced by Adam for the clients' previous home fitted in perfectly.

FAMILY TOWNHOUSE

Completely renovated in a scant twelve-week period before the client gave birth to twins, this city townhouse home was designed expressly to provide a calming backdrop to the chaos and noise of life with very young children.

These clients had first encountered Retrouvius when furnishing a home in Greece, for which they bought almost everything from the London warehouse, then had it shipped over there. A few years later, when they were expecting their first child, they asked Maria to design their apartment in central London. Four years down the line, they discovered that they were expecting twins, and realized that they needed to move into a larger space with some urgency. By the time they had access to their new home, there were only a few months left before the babies arrived in which to completely renovate and decorate the building.

Although no major structural work was required, almost every room in the house needed to be gutted, right down to the floors themselves. Getting a job of this size done on such a short timetable required almost superhuman effort on the part of everyone involved, including the clients.

THIS PAGE AND OPPOSITE The downstairs bathroom was papered in thick paper that had been destined for a special edition of the complete works of Shakespeare but had accidentally been sent through the presses twice. Although the double-printed pages were now useless to the Folio Society, the paper quality was too good to waste and thus perfect for salvaging. Most of the sheets in this room are from *The Taming of the Shrew*, which has apparently made for provocative, and indeed rather divisive, reading material for those using the bathroom.

The family who purchased their former apartment had a very different aesthetic and were not interested in keeping any elements of the existing décor. This pleased the client: "We loved our flat so much – we didn't want to leave, so it was great to be able to take some of it with us!" Before leaving the flat, materials such as the marble cladding in the bathroom were removed for use in the new home – so in effect, many of the materials redeployed in this house have been salvaged twice. That this was possible illustrates how important it is not to cut into good materials too much – installing materials in a way that renders them available for reuse in the future is an important part of the Retrouvius salvage philosophy.

All these beautiful materials are only available in limited quantities, so it is lovely to imagine that they will go on to have a long life. Of course, that doesn't mean that they have to be treated with kid gloves – the marks of age and use add their own richness to materials, and are attractive to clients such as these, who are sharing a house with three children under the age of four. "It's very childproof; I never worry about damaging things. It's one of the things that we enjoy – that we can live in the house and not be too precious about anything."

Salvaged parquet in two different woods was used for the floors of the entrance hall, sitting room and downstairs lavatory, and salvaged furniture features wherever possible, including a beautifully solid desk from a London museum and reconditioned bathroom fittings. A striped carpet on the stairs forms a dramatic focal point for the entrance hall and is picked up in striped

ABOVE AND OPPOSITE Rather than eating up a huge slab of the master bedroom with floor-to-ceiling fitted cupboards, a wardrobe unit was created that was just tall enough to hang a suit jacket. This left wall space free for artworks, and allowed the top of the unit to be used for display. A strip of drawer fronts salvaged from the Natural History Museum in Edinburgh were run across the front and side of the closet; these provide working handles for a drawer and for the cupboard doors. This theme of mixed surfaces was continued in the children's room (opposite). Here, the surface of the drawer fronts was broken up by different-coloured strips and a playful textural element was added by using old printer's letter blocks as handles on drawers that are at child-accessible height. A cosy slipper chair in vibrant yellow velvet completes the scene.

elements elsewhere in the house, such as the blind in the study and the bedroom storage units. Rather than engaging in a riot of colour, the children's bedrooms were kept calm and low key – as the client points out, the children make quite enough noise as it is, so the décor doesn't need to be loud as well.

Although they are not shown here, the clients' favourite rooms are the bathrooms. In the children's bathroom, Maria laid a strip of mirrored tiles above the edge of the bathtub. Little children tend to be fascinated by their own reflections, and the mirrors have proved a huge hit. All three children want to be in the tub at the same time, and the first thing that they do when they get in is kiss their own reflection. The floor and walls of the master bathroom were covered in Derbyshire fossil limestone to create a giant wet room, and it has become a family habit for everyone to converge there in the mornings. "The kids come in and play with their ducks in the bidet while I have a shower," says the client. "It's wonderful to have all the family in the bathroom – it's one of the few times that we're all together without fighting!"

With two rapidly growing children and a third one on the way, this family realized that they needed extra space, but felt happier trying to get as much as they could out of the house they were already living in rather than moving to somewhere new. The redesign had to draw together the needs of the various different characters sharing the house, and create a beautiful and dynamic space that could simultaneously accommodate yoga-loving creative bohemianism and 1950s Italian glamour, as well as the boundless energy of three small kids.

VICTORIAN VILLA

THIS PAGE AND OPPOSITE The marble used on the walls of the light, bright kitchen came from various sources. The pieces with gilt detailing on the end wall adjacent to the sliding doors to the garden (opposite) probably originated in a bank or office building and there was very little left; just a couple of slabs with a long gilt stripe and, intriguingly, the word "FIN". A sense of weightlessness was brought to the large kitchen island by facing one side with a mirror-glass panel that blurs the edges of the space and reflects even more light into the room.

Having knocked through the rooms on the ground floor to create one flowing living space, one of the two doors from the hall was replaced with a pane of glass faced with a flamboyant Rococo-style gate to prevent people from walking into it. Coming into the house, the first thing that you see is this gate and the light flooding through it from the glass doors at the back of the kitchen; the effect is both elegant and inviting. The curved wall that runs opposite (not pictured) was painted with a glossy finish, which gives a lovely textural contrast to the matte, rusted finish of the gate.

THIS PAGE AND OPPOSITE The newly opened-out ground floor was divided into two main zones. The sitting room area at the front is decorated in a palette of light and natural colours, and simple mid-century furnishings that allow the clients' artworks to provide focal bursts of colour. An eye-catching vertical bookcase, shelves full of artworks and objects kept safely out of toddler reach and a small upright piano all contribute to a space that feels at once culturally stimulating and intensely personal. The graphic 1950s wall lights add a touch of elegance to what is essentially quite a practical family space, and create dramatic shadows on the plain painted wall surfaces.

The main aim of the renovation was to open the house up as much as possible, allowing light to flood through from front to back, and creating extra space at the top and bottom. The major structural work involved excavating the basement to create a children's playroom, spare bedroom and bathroom and a little private recording studio.

With a new basement comes a new staircase. Rather than running it beneath the existing stairs at the front of the house, it was positioned to connect with the kitchen and living space further back. An arrangement like this is comforting for both children and parents. The children don't feel as though they are being shunted off to a distant chamber, and the parents can, to a certain extent, hear what's going on downstairs. The basement is a proper extension of the family space, fitting right into the heart of the home.

LEFT AND OPPOSITE BELOW RIGHT While the bedroom as a whole feels chic and luxurious, some of the individual elements are of surprisingly humble origin; the bedside tables are inexpensive pieces of mid-century wooden furniture repainted in complementary shades. Carrying a limited colour palette across disparate furniture pieces and through upholstery helps bring a sense of unity to objects and materials that reference different times and styles. The subtle shades also provide a backdrop for wilder flourishes, such as the exuberant 1950s wall lights (opposite below right) and the iridescent curtain fabric.

OPPOSITE ABOVE LEFT The starting point for the colour scheme in the master bedroom and dressing room was this Turkish rug, which provided a remarkable palette of duck-egg blue, lavender and dusty cocoa.

OPPOSITE ABOVE RIGHT Space was stolen back from a former dressing room to create an office space on the landing, hidden by a curtain and with a beautiful long axial view out over the street.

The client has a serious interest in cooking, and with three children to feed, the kitchen needed to be a hardworking space, so all the more reason to fill it with rich and satisfyingly solid materials: marble, slate, mirror, wood and worn leather. Many of the design choices within this space were dictated by the limitations that come from using salvaged materials. For example, the piece of marble used for the worksurface of the unit that backs onto the staircase was not quite deep enough, so a piece of wood had to be added to increase the depth. This created a patchwork quality that was added to by running a line of small tiles along the bottom of the wood pane, resulting in a lovely visual detail on the back of the unit that breaks up what could otherwise have been a slab of white wall in the middle of the living space.

The big wooden kitchen unit had been salvaged in a very bad state from an old draper's shop. The drawers were given new runners and a worksurface was created from a slab of hardwood from a science lab. The marble on the kitchen walls is from a variety of different sources. The eighteenth-century chimneybreast roundels were found in a former stonemason's yard and had been waiting in the Retrouvius warehouse for the right home. The marble slabs with gilt detailing probably originated in a bank or grand office building.

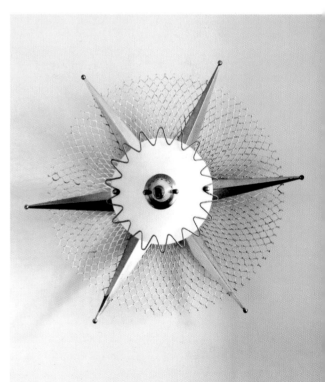

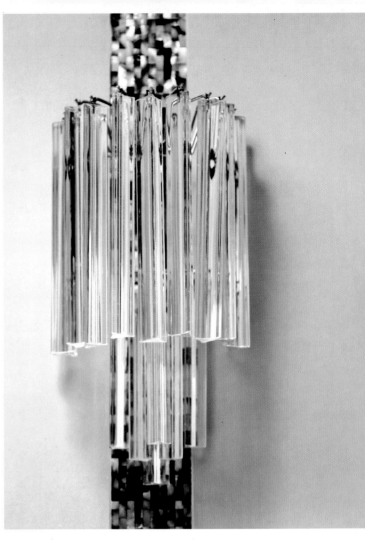

Working with salvage isn't just about reclaimed materials; it's also about reusing materials on site. The wooden cladding in the spare room in the basement was put together from the house's existing floorboards. Space was used for maximum efficiency – a nook for a little curtained-off office was stolen from a cupboard on the landing, and a treehouse-style hideout was created between two of the boys' bedrooms and tucked under the ridge of the roof. This clever use of awkward spaces and the attention to the flow of light allows other parts of the house, such as the master bedroom and living room, to feel spacious and airy, while in truth a great many different functions are being packed into a relatively compact space.

THIS PAGE AND OPPOSITE The master bathroom combines a hint of Art Deco elegance with practical modernity. The contemporary double walk-in shower and salvaged bathtub are both backed by handmade off-white tiles that bring continuity to the space. The grey tones in the tiles echo the marble surfaces of the reconditioned French double basin. The beautiful glass 1950s wall lamp above the sinks anchors the elegant look. When using a chic feature like this as an imaginative bathroom fitting, it is important to adapt the wiring to make sure that the bulb can work safely in damp conditions.

THIS PAGE AND OPPOSITE Inspired by William Morris's interest in ancient buildings, Maria often uses textiles architecturally. When backed by natural contemporary fabrics such as linen, salvaged textile fragments can become strong enough for active use in the home. The gorgeous embroidered panel of a stork (opposite) forms the centrepiece in a hallway, dividing the space and imbuing it with warmth. This Chinese panel (right) was picked up by a client in a junk shop, and incorporated into a curtain that acts as a door in the large aperture between the kitchen and the rest of the house. The heavy quilted patchwork of these bedroom curtains (below right) makes them an effective blackout for a night owl who likes his sleep.

MATERIAL PROFILE: FABRIC

Textiles play a key role in the Retrouvius design style, and Maria often takes a vintage rug, tapestry or piece of embroidery as the foundation for the palette of a room. Referring to the colours of the fabric in upholstery and paintwork can draw a room together and create a common thread through disparate styles of furniture.

For many of the projects in this book, Retrouvius collaborated with textile specialists Kirsten Hecktermann and Lucy Bathurst. "All the backcloths to go with antique textiles will be linen or cotton; natural textiles that are as close as you can get to the original," explains Lucy. "It all has to be hand stitched – old pieces are not square, and tend not to lie flat." Salvaged textiles not only have the subtlety to complement the interior of a very old home and soften the impact of new furniture but they can also be used to strikingly modern effect, for example in the geometric panels of Lucy's lace-embellished blind (see pages 72–73). This Mondrian-like design, stitched from scraps of handmade trimming, was inspired by a trip to Denmark, where Maria photographed sunlight shining through lace curtains and casting a shadow on the floor.

LEFT AND RIGHT This richly coloured tapestry featuring birds, vegetables and butterflies (left) was designed by French artist Jean Lurçat. The dominant tones of ochre, rust and umber are picked up throughout the home, for example in the upholstery of the Poul Kjaerholm daybed seen in front of it. The colours are in contrast to the cool coffee and cream graphic featured on the original carpet, (right) tiles and upholstery.

High above London, this apartment is a classic piece of 1970s design that has had to adapt to accommodate antique furniture, small children and a couple with very strong aesthetic sensibilities of their own.

HIGH-RISE HOME

Looking out on one side through deep windows under the eaves of a central London mansion block, and on the other through sliding glass doors onto an enclosed garden, this L-shaped rooftop apartment was designed in 1973 by Adam's father, the architect Nicholas Hills. Although he had a young family at the time, it was not intended as a family home – more the kind of place that you would refer to as a 'pad' (as in bachelor) rather than a 'home' (as in family). Certainly the bespoke carpet, tiles and fabric, with their geometric coffee and cream stripes, now seem the acme of 1970s glamour.

THIS PAGE AND OPPOSITE The L-shaped living space wraps around a rooftop garden, and allows for long vistas through segments of the home; in this case (above) all the way along the sitting room and into the kitchen. The shower room (seen right) leads directly off the kitchen, and is clad in fossil limestone salvaged from Heathrow Airport. The same limestone is also used in the Royal Festival Hall; Maria describes it as "the stone that epitomizes post-war British architecture". The kitchen tabletop (opposite) is a slab of reclaimed walnut – it's rare to find a sizeable piece like this.

There is, of course, nothing more apt to set the teeth on edge than the styles of the recent past. When Adam and Maria moved into the flat in 1997, it was, to say the least, with mixed feelings. Having started their architectural salvage practice in Glasgow, focusing on conservation-led work with Victorian and ecclesiastical architecture, it was a bit of a rude shock to arrive in "what felt like a grubby, moth-eaten and rather tired space".

As it turns out, their architectural history professor from Glasgow had visited the flat in the late 1970s. "When he heard we were moving back in he said 'you must NOT get rid of that carpet'," recalls Maria. "I'm quite grateful that he did make us work with and live with it. I like it when I have to be sensitive to

what already exists." More than fifteen years later, the carpet is down to its last fibres, but it will live on in eternal memory as the backdrop to most of the children's baby photographs.

In many ways, moving into this aluminium and glass-sided flat with its white walls and coordinated aesthetic marked a turning point in Adam and Maria's working life. "We moved in just as *Wallpaper** magazine was launched," explains Adam. "After our strict conservation background in Glasgow, suddenly being in a 1970s slightly louche place, just at that point where retro-modern furniture suddenly became *de rigeur*, it was really liberating to be able to adjust our focus in salvage into a modern idiom. In Glasgow it had all been about restoring old buildings,

RIGHT AND OPPOSITE Adam and Maria's own home has become an invaluable testing ground for their understanding of how a home can evolve to meet the changing needs of a family. Their apartment is now arranged to cater for their children, with much of the furniture displaying a low centre of gravity that works well for parents playing with children on the floor.

but in London I became interested in saving materials and the possibility of reuse."

Maria was particularly interested in the flexibility of the space – she has moved every piece of furniture into every possible configuration and, over the years, slept in every part of the flat as it evolved from being a hybrid business and living space, through to being home to one and then two children. "It was originally designed for what Modernism was meant to be about," she explains; "flexibility and the possibility of change."

While the structural aesthetic of the flat has been left largely untouched, with two young children came the need for a new, larger kitchen, which turned into a glorious hymn to salvaged materials. The marble countertop came from their local fishmonger who shut up shop a couple of years ago; it is an enormous slab of marble that once served as a display shelf in the shop window. The dining table is topped with a huge, beautiful piece of reclaimed walnut wood and has old Belgian tubular framed school chairs set around it.

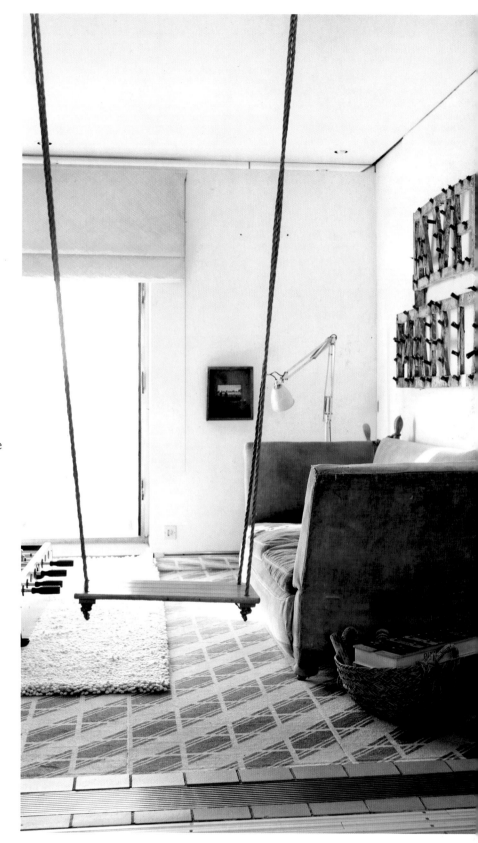

THIS PAGE AND OPPOSITE Like many of their clients, Adam and Maria share space with furniture inherited from relatives, or brought from a previous home with a very different architectural language. They have had to learn how to negotiate between the different forms and styles. Often textiles and colour can be used to create a link between pieces that otherwise have little in common. The bench and table (opposite) are united by their yellow painted bases. The panels on the wall (detail below) are glass drawer backs from the Victoria and Albert Museum and were originally used for storing textile fragments.

The kitchen walls are clad in teak strip flooring reclaimed from an army barracks. "It looks terrible when it comes into the warehouse," explains Maria. "Like it should go straight onto a bonfire." The pieces on the walls have been hand sanded to keep the patina and irregular surface, while those used for the doors of the shower room and guest bedroom have been put through a belt sander that leaves them dead flat but with the beautiful glow of old wood.

The kitchen wall light was found by Adam and shows no maker's mark of any kind — he thinks it may have been a working prototype, or just a piece made with available parts, but the colours and shapes of the lampshades have made it one of the few salvaged pieces from

the warehouse that they have decided to hang onto (the other two being the Lurçat tapestry and the charcoal drawings in their bedroom). The kitchen units were given an aluminium front that picks up on the structure of the building and acts as a link between the reclaimed materials and the structure they occupy.

As well as accommodating all the chaos and clutter that life with young children seems to involve, the apartment has also recently absorbed a large quantity of furniture from Adam's grandfather. "If you came here five years ago, you would have seen Joe Colombo chairs – now it's all Georgian and Victorian" says Maria. However, the open spaces of the flat mean that these pieces can be given plenty of room to 'breathe' aesthetically, rather than being crammed up against each other. The glass walls also resist any inclination to shuffle furniture away

OPPOSITE Here, as in many of Maria's design projects, a striking textile piece acts as the foundation for the rest of the room. In this case, it is the printed fabric used on the bed headboard, which, like the tapestry on the living room wall, was designed by Jean Lurçat. The olive green colour used within the print is extended across the headboard and picked up in the upholstery of the two armchairs. **RIGHT** On the bedroom wall are two eighteenth-century French charcoal drawings discovered folded up at an antiques fair, and one of the few finds kept out of the warehouse.

around the side of a room. By using salvaged materials in a modern way, visual echoes are created between, for example, a Victorian clock and armchair and the reclaimed hardwood used in an office unit.

The home is, in many ways, very different from Maria's design projects. As a kind of never-ending work in progress, however, it has turned into a testing ground for ideas about how the spaces of a home function in family life. While perhaps not a perfect aesthetic reflection of Retrouvius's practice, it is very much a philosophical reflection of it, of the sensitivity towards existing architectural language, of a human-led architectural practice, of the thoughtfulness towards the needs of children in a home and the acceptance that the design of an interior is not a stable, rigid thing, but something that moves, flows and builds over time.

The coffee and cream-coloured striped graphic used on the carpet, tiles and curtains throughout the flat was designed by Adam's father, the architect Nicholas Hills, who built the rooftop apartment in 1973. After nearly forty years of use, the carpet is, alas, rather threadbare. The sunken bathtub (left) was originally echoed in height and form by the Poul Kjaerholm daybed (see pages 120–121), which sat opposite. While conceived as part of a rather suggestive bathroom arrangement, it actually worked brilliantly for parents bathing young children, and has inspired Maria to include low seats and daybeds in a number of her bathroom designs.

LEFT AND RIGHT Rather than adding a door between the sitting room and the office, a long curtain pole was mounted on the wall, and a panel of Emery & Cie's richly decorative Méchants Oiseaux fabric was suspended from it. The dark colour brings warmth to the room in the evenings, and the thickness of the fabric helps keep the heat of the adjacent stove in the space. Raw linens from Fran White's The Linen Shop were used for the curtains and blinds, and old French sheets to upholster the contemporary daybed (right) to help it blend in with the vintage beech wood furniture elsewhere in the room.

Set above rolling parkland to the south of the Chiltern Hills in an area once famous for its beech forests, this barn conversion was the first stage in a major building project. Now housing a games room, study and spare bedroom, The Byre was originally an old farm building containing a stable, cowshed and workshop.

REFURBISHED BARN

The design of this barn has a natural, airy quality to it, with much of the colour palette provided by beautiful raw materials, many of which have a rather noble or ancient aspect to them. There is, of course, considerable illusion at play here; although the materials are indeed old and wonderful, most of them were salvaged from other sites and brought into the building, then combined with contemporary elements to create a design that appears intrinsic to the space, yet has all the warmth, practicality and energy efficiency of a modern building.

The balancing act in this project was to adhere to good environmental practice without interfering too much with the style and fabric of the building. Insulation was added to the roof, floors and walls, and an air-source heat pump was installed (although this has not, alas, been an unqualified triumph).

The wood panels at the far end of this room conceal cupboards and a television. The oak boards were edged with a trim of salvaged hardwood, and a strip running vertically up the sliding door creates an abstract pattern on the wood, making its concealed function less apparent.

THIS PAGE AND OPPOSITE
The interior takes its colour palette from a handful of raw materials; the walls are finished in lime plaster, which gives a textured finish that does not need to be painted. Salvaged oak floorboards were used for the bedroom floor, the lower half of the back walls in the bedroom and living room and to face the storage units. The flooring in the rest of the building uses cut bricks, the colours of which are echoed in the plaster-toned Delft tiles along the bottom of the walls, and stone-coloured Zellige tiles in the bathroom.

In order to keep the original ceiling joists and boards visible, insulation was built up on the outside, then a slate roof placed over it. Natural materials, such as lime plaster, linen and reclaimed wood, were used throughout – not only are they environmentally friendly but they also fit the ancient rusticity of the barn.

The original flooring was made up of cobbles, but they were deemed too uneven for a workable floor and were removed for use in the garden. The new flooring is made up of old cut brick. When working with a material like this, Maria is always conscious of wastage; Retrouvius look at salvaged materials as valuable not just to the current owners but to whoever comes to use them in the future. Subtle adjustments to the way materials are used can make a big difference; for example, laying cut bricks such as these in a herringbone pattern would have required a large number of bricks to be cut at angles to accommodate the shape of the

room, which would ultimately have been wasteful. Laying the bricks in a stack bond or running bond pattern instead ensures that as little as possible of the material is cut into.

Most of the storage space in the bedroom and living room is concealed in the dividing wall between the two spaces, which is faced in oak boards on both sides, panels of which slide or swing open to reveal cupboards, drawers and even a flat-screen TV.

The beech forests that used to cover this area were once the foundation of a flourishing furniture trade (the local football team is still known as The Chair Boys). Little of this remains today save for Ercol, a company started in 1920 and that rose to prominence with its innovative bentwood furniture in the 1940s and '50s. In tribute to the local connection, the sitting room has been furnished with an old Ercol coffee table and Ercol chairs upholstered in Hungarian linen.

GEORGIAN FARMHOUSE

This farmhouse had been patched and extended
into a rather awkward structure over the years.
The redesign brings out the best of its handsome
proportions, and transforms it into a warm family
home flooded with light and views of the garden.

Prior to the renovation, this house had evolved into a rather peculiar L-shape.
The central Georgian section of the building had been clumsily extended in
the early twentieth century, leaving the front door hidden in a corner of the
building, which felt rather unwelcoming. To create a more pleasing structure, a
new extension was built to fill in the angle of the 'L', turning what seemed like a
smallish house into a very spacious home and transforming a higgledy-piggledy
building into a grand farmhouse with Georgian proportions.

LEFT AND RIGHT This hallway window
(seen both left and right) was one of
the few remaining well-preserved
features of the original Georgian
building that forms the core of this
house. It was kept intact partly to
maintain a historical link to the
architecture of the house and partly
to let light into the hallway from the
room beyond. The window also
allows visitors to intuitively
understand how the house is
arranged – the line of sight leads
them straight through into the two
big reception rooms. A mirror above
the fireplace opposite the window
bounces the light back into the
space again.

"I chose the house because it's light, and I loved all the windows," explains the client. "There was enough room to feel that there was space for everyone, but there was also a heart to it. It had a very strong sense of being a family home." The strong heart of the home was developed by the creation of long vistas through the ground floor. The side door leading on to the kitchen was the one most used by the family. It was centred by two metres (seven feet), so that on entering the house you can look through the kitchen, into the hall and right through the reception rooms to a lovely arched window at the other end of the house.

Wherever you are in the house, there is a visual connection to the outside world. Spaces were opened up all over the building to allow the natural light to flood in. The original Georgian window in the hallway has remained in place, even though the new extension was built around it, and it now opens onto the sitting room beyond.

the upholstery of the Van Duysen sofas. The colour is also echoed in the tiles surrounding the fireplace on the opposite wall in the front reception room (see overleaf). When furnishing an old country house, it's important to have a certain proportion of the contents looking lived in right from the beginning. The beautiful rug was chosen to give the room a pleasantly worn-in feel. The tapestry panel just seen on the far left is mounted on a set of runners and slides back to reveal a flat-screen television.

LEFT AND BELOW LEFT The trim on these curtains is an early form of crewelwork, a single strip of which was found by Maria on a very early morning visit to Kempton Park antiques market. The embroidery is fragile and a little damaged, but the gaps in the pattern bring their own aesthetic, making the fabric look rather abstract and modern in its design.
OPPOSITE These copper light doors were salvaged by Adam from the University of the Arts building near Bond Street in central London. The building was being demolished to make way for the Crossrail development. Adam was tipped off by someone who worked in the building and bought sixty pairs of doors from the demolition company. Retrouvius like these doors and windows so much that they have actually constructed the façade of their warehouse from them. Here they have been mounted to slide into pockets in the wall between the two reception rooms.

There are also references to the natural world throughout the house, from the magnificent stork embroidery in the entrance hall (see pages 138-139), to wallpaper featuring birds and flowers, and textiles featuring butterflies, chicken and sheep. This constant reminder of the outdoors came from the client. "I was keen to have this sense of the outside – which is where I feel most comfortable – inside," she explains. "The garden is very important to me, and a lot of the themes within the house are also developing in the garden."

Because the family is still young, Maria put great thought into keeping the spaces flexible, so that the home can evolve as the children grow. While the house is designed to be as open plan as possible, sliding doors between some rooms mean that the space can be divided or joined up as needed, to give play space or privacy. The attic playroom is already wired for a television and computer, in order to become a den or extra bedroom.

OPPOSITE The client had really wanted to keep the original floorboards in this little book room but, alas, much of the wood was rotten and not suitable for reuse within the house. Whatever could be salvaged has been stored on site and will be used in the garden. The replacement floorboards came from an army barracks.

With much of the house, the aim was to use salvaged materials to keep things looking as authentic as possible. Floorboards from an army barracks replaced those that had rotted away or were no longer fit for use. Beautiful but worn rugs and textiles in the reception room look as though they have always been there and keep the mood relaxed. A grand entrance hall was created, fronted by a salvaged Georgian door complete with fluted pilasters and fanlight window above. This was placed in a position formerly occupied by a window and the original boxing around the window frame was kept and extended so that the new door blends into the architecture of the house.

Although the staircase at the back of the hall is not especially large, because it now leads onto the back of the entrance hall, its position immediately gives it an air of significance. The entrance hall feels rich and inviting; guests are greeted by a gold and red embroidered panel featuring an orientalized stork motif that hangs across the hall (see pages 138–139). The embroidery brings both visual and

THIS PAGE While the house feels like a very open and enveloping family space, Maria created lots of special hidden-away spaces and niches – like this window seat – which allow for moments of quiet and contemplation. Spaces such as these offer little oases of peace and privacy at the same time as being connected to everything else that's happening in the home.

LEFT Because it is positioned to one side of the room, this very large dining table still manages to look relatively informal. Benches were built in along the wall on two sides, which makes it very flexible for everyday use and ideal for children.
OPPOSITE In the dining room, the floor-length curtains feature a panel of South African textile found by the client. The upholstery fabric on the armchair is Moroccan, as is the rag rug.

actual warmth to the hallway, blocking draughts and counterbalancing the antique greys of the paintwork. The reception rooms are visible through the interior window, and because the space has been opened out, even first-time visitors have an immediate sense of how the house fits together.

The reception rooms are led by cerulean blues and rich reds, dominated at one end by an old Royal Doulton ceramic fireplace (see pages 140–141), and at the other by a chimney breast covered in similarly toned blue-green Zellige tiles. The bench and fire surround is made from cast concrete that has been needled to take off the surface and expose the aggregate so that it doesn't look too slick and finished. "Maria is amazing at listening to what you want," says the client. "Her natural colour palette and mine are very different – I'm much more interested in blues and reds, while she loves greens and ochres. But she'll always come back with ideas that sit comfortably with me, and makes them look amazing."

The little book room at the back of the ground floor features a panel of old French wallpaper, of which Maria only found one roll. An extra door was installed here, to create a new route around the ground floor, and the children now enjoy running in circles between the kitchen, hallway and book room. The new door has brought life to what

LEFT AND ABOVE In the kitchen, Maria used shelves to divide the cooking and dining areas. They act as a screen and allow whoever is cooking a modicum of privacy. The cast-iron brackets of the shelves came from the Patent Office. They were fitted with new shelves made from boards that had previously been used for maturing cheese.

was a little-used room in the house and helps everything to feel more flowing and spacious.

The old family Aga was kept in the kitchen, converted from oil to gas (which has made it more efficient and a lot less smelly) and refurbished. A new floor made from a mixture of pinkish Jerusalem stone and limestone found by the client was put down, and a new kitchen was installed. All the units in the kitchen are fronted with salvaged oak panels that were once drawer bottoms in the Natural History Museum in London. While the kitchen doesn't look like a conventional fitted kitchen, because the panelling has been used

throughout, it is impossible to distinguish between drawers, cupboards and appliances. The overlapping lips of the panels also act as the handles on the drawers and kitchen units.

Climbing the stairs to the first floor, you are met by a large landing space that was once an additional bedroom but has now been opened up all the way to a window at the front of the building. This area houses a comfortable armchair and a football table, and provides a great play area for the children at the beginning and end of the day. "Maria described it to us as somewhere that we'd play a lot after bath times, and she's so right – we have such a laugh up there; we all play table football or read. It has worked out really well as a relaxed family space," says the client.

THIS PAGE AND OPPOSITE Nature motifs feature throughout this home, reflecting the client's love of the natural world. The bird pattern wallpaper in the guest bathroom (opposite) is old wallpaper salvaged by Maria. In the dressing room (this page), the salvaged oak panels that form the wardrobe doors feature a laser-etched bird design by Daniel Heath.

ABOVE RIGHT The first floor of the house had originally been arranged as a series of rooms off a tiny corridor. When the house was extended, one of the existing bedrooms was knocked through to create an open space that broke free from the cramped corridor feeling. This space has now become a great congregation point for the family after the children's bath time, and helps to keep the home feeling light and airy.

LEFT, ABOVE LEFT AND OPPOSITE Colourful boards salvaged from a gymnasium floor were used as a recurring design element throughout the house. They came in a variety of finishes and colours, and when rearranged to fit onto the walls, they create a random yet pleasing stripy effect.

The bedrooms and bathrooms have a very child-focused design, including cheerful yet stylish textiles and wallpapers featuring animals and birds. There is a special low basin for the children to use, and a railway carriage luggage rack for their towels.

The grown-ups' quarters are rich with a mixture of old lace and textiles picked up by Maria at antiques fairs, wooden boards from a gymnasium floor that were left deliberately mismatched and scuffed, and sophisticated contemporary tiles and fabrics, including a flying dove pattern used on the headboard in the master bedroom by the zoological illustrator Mark Hearld.

The client admits that she found it very difficult watching the process that the house went through during renovation – improving the insulation, treating damp and removing rotten boards are very intrusive to the fabric of a building. At one point, though, the old plaster came off to reveal little pieces of a very beautiful old wallpaper, which she has kept to turn into a picture as a memento.

STOCKISTS AND SUPPLIERS

Design and Architectural

Brenzinger & Bartelt Architekten

Maximilianstrasse 36
79100 Freiburg
Germany
www.brenziger-bartelt.com
+49 (0)761 70596542
Architect for the project shown on pages 64–73

Retrouvius Design Ltd

2a Ravensworth Road
London NW10 5NR
www.retrouvius.com
+44 (0)20 8960 6060

Retrouvius Reclamation Ltd

2a Ravensworth Road
London NW10 5NR
www.retrouvius.com
+44 (0)20 8960 6060

Charles Tashima Architect

www.ct-arch.co.uk
+44 (0)207 281 23 51
Architect for the project shown on pages 40–51.

Textiles, wallpapers and fittings

Lucy Bathurst Nest Design

+44 (0)20 7794 9698
lucy@nestdesign.co.uk
www.nestdesign.co.uk
Textile designer using antique and salvaged textiles.

Bent Ply

95 Lisson Grove
London NW1 6UP
www.bentply.com
+44 (0)20 7725 9515
Twentieth-century furniture, lighting, rugs and objects.

The Claremont Furnishing Fabrics Company

35 Elystan Street
London SW3 3NT
+44 (0)20 7581 9575
www.claremontfurnishing.com
Specialist textiles and trimmings, stores in London, New York and Los Angeles.

Colonial Wall Coverings

707 East Passyunk Avenue
Philadelphia, PA 19147
+ 1 215 687-6457
www.colonialwallcoverings.com
Boutique wallpapers, including designs by Daniel Heath.

Thomas Crapper & Co Ltd

The Stable Yard
Ascot Park
Stratford-on–Avon
Warwickshire CV37 8BL
+44 (0)1789 450 522
www.thomas-crapper.com
Authentic period-style sanitaryware.

Neisha Crosland

+44 (0)20 7657 1150
www.neishacrosland.com
Available in the US from:
Clarence House
D&D Building
979 Third Ave, Suite 205
New York, NY 10022
+ 1 212 752 2890
www.clarencehouse.com
Fabric and wallpaper designer.

Aiveen Daly

2 Letchford Gardens
London NW10 6AS
(by appointment only)
+44 (0) 208 962 0044
www.aiveendaly.com
Furniture and soft furnishings

Dashing Tweeds

5 St. Mark's Crescent
London NW1 7TS
(by appointment only)
www.dashingtweeds.co.uk
Textile company using the best of British mills and workshops to create classic quality tweeds and accessories.

Desousa Hughes

San Francisco Design Center
2 Henry Adams Street
Showroom 220
San Francisco, CA 94103
+ 1 415 626 6883
www.desousahughes.com
Glamorous wallcoverings, including designs by Timorous Beasties.

Hugh Dunford Wood

Little Place
Silver Street
Lyme Regis
Dorset DT7 3HB
+44 (0)1297 442 121
www.handmadewallpaper.co.uk
Hand-blocked printed papers, bespoke colours.

Emery & Cie

78 Quai des Charbonnages
1080 Brussels
+32 2 513 58 92
www.emeryetcie.com
Visit the website for details of their showrooms in Paris, Antwerp and Brussels. Available in London exclusively from the Retrouvius warehouse (by appointment only).
Belgian designer Agnès Emery regularly conjures up beautifully vibrant colour palettes. Wallpaper, fabrics, rugs, tiles, lighting and paints.

Daniel Heath

www.danielheath.co.uk
London-based maker of bespoke silkscreen-printed fabrics and hand-printed wallpapers.

Kirsten Hecktermann

+44 (0)788 768 0672
www.kirstenhecktermann.com
Textile artist producing hand-dyed velvets and hand-painted fabrics. The Retrouvius warehouse stocks a selection of her latest cushions.

Larusi

Unit 14, The Dove Centre
109 Bartholomew Road
London NW5 2BJ
(by appointment only)
+44 (0)207 428 0256
www.larusi.com
Tribal rugs and textiles.

Matter Matters

405 Broome Street
New York, NY 10013
+ 1 212 343 2600
www.mattermatters.com
Furniture and fittings, including wallpapers by Timorous Beasties.

Michelle Oberdieck

Oxo Tower Unit 1.04
Bargehouse Street
London SE1 9PH
www.micheleoberdieck.co.uk
Textile and glass artist, producing glass panels and printed fabrics.

Ochre

462 Broome Street
New York, NY 10013
+1 212 414 4332
www.ochrestore.com
Vintage and organic textiles, ceramics, glassware and baskets.

Sue Skeen

sueskeen@btinternet.com
Stylist and painter. Enquiries by email only.

Timorous Beasties

46 Amwell Street
London EC1R 1XS
+44 (0)20 7833 5010
and at
384 Great Western Road
Glasgow G4 9HT
+44 (0)141 337 2622
www.timorousbeasties.com
Wallpaper and textile designers.

Walnut Wallpaper

7424 Beverly Bvld
Los Angeles, CA 90036
+1 323 932 9166
www.walnutwallpaper.com
The best of wallpaper and fabric designs, including those by Timorous Beasties, as well as vintage offerings.

Antiques dealers and salvage yards

Alscot

+44 (0)121 709 0266.
www.alscotbathrooms.com
Suppliers and restorers of original antique bathrooms.

Ardingly

International antiques and collectors fair
www.iacf.co.uk
South-east England's largest antiques and collectors fair, held 6 times a year.

Hein Bonger

22 High Street
Saxmundham
Suffolk IP17 1AJ
+44 (0)1728 604 382
Reclaimed furniture.

Dix Sept Antiques

17 Station Road
Framlingham
Suffolk IP13 9EA
+44 (0)1728 621505
An eclectic mix of furniture and items for the house and garden.

Historic Houseparts

540 South Avenue
Rochester, NY 14620
+1 585 325 2329
www.historichouseparts.com
Salvaged doors, sinks, and tiles.

Kempton Antiques Fair

www.sunburyantiques.com
Britain's largest antiques and collectors fair, held twice monthly.

Leominster Reclamation Ltd

North Road
Leominster
Herefordshire HR6 0AB
www.leorec.co.uk
+44 (0)1568 616 205
Architectural salvage and reclaimed building materials.

Max Inc

Sharaz Karim
106 Askew Road
London W12 9BL
+44 (0)7973 121 879
www.maxinc.co.uk
Vintage lights & furniture.

Mongers Architectural Salvage

15 Market Place
Hingham
Norfolk NR9 4AF
+44 (0)1953 851 868.
www.mongersofhingham.co.uk
Reclaimed sanitary ware, fireplaces, doors, windows and architectural features.

Olde Good Things

Union Square
5 East 16th Street
New York, NY 10003
+1 212 989 8814
www.ogtstore.com
Architectural salvage.

Olliff's Architectural Salvage

St Werburgs Road
Bristol BS2 9XZ
www.olliffs.com
Architectural antiques.

SALVO

All enquires through website:
www.salvo.co.uk
A directory of architectural salvage suppliers.

Trouver Antiques

59 South Hill Park
London NW3 2SS
+44 (0)7973 885 671
www.trouverantiques.co.uk
English and French furniture.

Interesting societies

Ancient Monuments Society

St Ann's Vestry Hall
2 Church Entry
London EC4V 5HB
+44 (0)207 236 3934
www.ancientmonumentssociety.org.uk
Society for the study and conservation of ancient monuments, historic buildings and fine old craftsmanship.

The Twentieth Century Society

70 Cowcross Street
London EC1M 6EJ
www.c20society.org.uk
Society campaigning for the preservation of Britain's architectural heritage.

Victorian Society

1 Priory Gardens
London W4 1TT
+44 (0)208 994 1019
www.victoriansociety.org.uk
Society championing Victorian and Edwardian buildings.

Other nice things we enjoy

Clouds Hill

Wareham BH20 7NQ
+44 (0)1929 405616
www.nationaltrust.org.uk/clouds-hill
The home of T. E. Lawrence, now owned by the National Trust.

Coco Maya

12 Connaught St
London W2 2AF
+44 (0)20 7706 2883
www.cocomaya.co.uk
Fine chocolatier and artisan baker.

The George in Rye

98 High Street, Rye
East Sussex TN31 7JT
+44 (0)1797 222114
www.thegeorgeinrye.com
Fabulous hotel in Rye with individually designed rooms by Retrouvius – a great chance to experience Retrouvius design at first hand.

Kelmscott Manor

Kelmscott
Lechlade
Oxfordshire GL7 3HJ
www.kelmscottmanor.org.uk
The country home of William Morris, now owned and run by the Society of Antiquaries.

Kettle's Yard

Castle Street
Cambridge CB3 0AQ
+44 (0)1223 748100
www.kettlesyard.co.uk
Beautiful and unique Cambridge art gallery.

Little Angel Puppet Theatre

14 Dagmar Passage
London N1 2DN
+44 (0)20 7226 1787
www.littleangeltheatre.com
London puppet theatre.

The Town Mill Bakery

2 Coombe Street
Lyme Regis
Dorset DT7 3PY
+44 (0)1297 444754
www.townmillbakery.com
Organic artisan bakers.

BUSINESS CREDITS

Retrouvius
2A Ravensworth Road
Kensal Green
London NW10 5NR
+44 (0)20 8960 6060
E: design@retrouvius.com
www.retrouvius.com

*Pages: endpapers; 2; 6–15; 39
above right; 39 below; 62; 63
above right; 80; 81 above and
below right; 120 -131.*

Architect Charles Tashima
www.ct-arch.co.uk
+44 (0)207 281 23 51
Pages 40–51.

**Architect Annika Dyllick
Brenzinger**
**Brenzinger & Bartelt
Architekten**
Maximilianstrasse 36
79100 Freiburg
Germany
+49 (0)761 70596542
www.brenzinger-bartelt.com
Pages 102–107.

Catherine Johnson
Interior Design Consultancy
By appointment
cat.whitehead@btinternet.com
+41 79 463 12 95
Pages 64–73.

Guys Hills
Dashing Tweeds
By appointment at:
5 St. Mark's Crescent
London NW1 7TS
+44 (0)20 7267 3352
Mobile: +44 (0)7831 548068
E: guy@dashingtweeds.co.uk
www.dashingtweeds.co.uk

*Pages 4 left and below right;
26–37; 63 above left.*

PICTURE CREDITS

Endpapers: the Retrouvius warehouse; **1** The home of George Lamb in London; **2** Retrouvius owners Adam Hills and Maria Speake's apartment in London; **3** The home of James and Marisa Backhouse in London; **4 left and below right** The home of Guy and Natasha Hills in London; **5** The home of James and Marisa Backhouse in London; **6–15** The Retrouvius warehouse; **16–25** The home of James and Marisa Backhouse in London; **26–37** The home of Guy and Natasha Hills in London; **39 above right** Retrouvius owners Adam Hills and Maria Speake's apartment in London; **39 below** the Retrouvius warehouse; **52–61** The home of George Lamb in London; **62 and 63 above right** the Retrouvius warehouse; **63 above left** The home of Guy and Natasha Hills in London; **63 below** The home of James and Marisa Backhouse in London; **80** the Retrouvius warehouse; **81 above right** Retrouvius owners Adam Hills and Maria Speake's apartment in London; **81 below right** the Retrouvius warehouse; **102–107** The home of Elina Tripoliti and Mark Rachovides in London; **119 below** The home of George Lamb in London; **120–131** Retrouvius owners Adam Hills and Maria Speake's apartment in London.

INDEX

Figures in *italics* indicate captions.

ACKNOWLEDGMENTS

We are grateful to RPS staff (both past and present) for giving us the excuse and opportunity to collate this first book of our work. Particular thanks go to Alison Starling for initiating, and to Cindy Richards, Annabel Morgan, Leslie Harrington, Megan Smith and Jess Walton for being so warm, friendly and sympathetic to our whims.

The Retrouvius design team who have worked on these projects so organically include James Stevens, Anthi Grapsa, Annika Brenzinger, Holger Schwarz, Pippa Small, Lucy Bathurst, Harriet Hodgson, Nicholas Hughes, Toby Hart and James Faulconer. All other members of the Retrouvius reclamation team are also thanked for their enthusiasm and help managing the warehouse with its ever-changing materials and oddities.

Thanks to Hettie Judah for eloquently interpreting our thoughts, and Debi Treloar for maintaining professionalism whilst coping with Maria's various crises (and always wearing inspiring outfits).

We are indebted to all the demolishers, dealers and suppliers who have fed us the raw materials that contributed to these projects, and the contractors who have worked their magic. In particular, Mick – you are a star.

We are incredibly appreciative of our clients (you know who you are) for having faith and entrusting their homes and souls into our hands.

Biggest thanks to our two boys Marcus and Hal for their good nature and joyous outlook on life.